OUR ORGANIZATION

Books by Brian O'Connell

Walker and Company:

Finding Values that Work: The Search for Fulfillment
Effective Leadership in Voluntary Organizations (paperback ed.)
Our Organization

The Foundation Center:

America's Voluntary Spirit
The Board Member's Book
Philanthropy in Action

OUR ORGANIZATION

Brian O'Connell

WALKER & COMPANY, NEW YORK

First published in the United States of America
in 1987 by the Walker Publishing Company, Inc.

Published simultaneously in Canada by Thomas Allen & Son
Canada, Limited, Markham, Ontario

Library of Congress Cataloging-in-Publication Data

O'Connell, Brian, 1930–
  Our organization / by Brian O'Connell.
    p.   cm.
  1. Associations, institutions, etc.—United States—Anecdotes,
facetiae, satire, etc. I. Title.
AS911.A2025 1987
367'.0207—dc19   87-17196
                                                        CIP

ISBN 0-8027-1006-9

Printed in the United States of America

10 9 8 7 6 5 4 3 2 1

TO THE VOLUNTEERS

*You Are Such a Wonderful Part
Of the Fabric and Spirit of America*

<u>Any</u> resemblance to <u>any</u> board member with whom I have ever worked is an unbelievable coincidence.

Roster of Participants

Rodney Russell,
  Chairperson
Penelope Mitchell,
  Vice Chairperson
Mrs. Jeffrey (Effie) Black,
  Secretary
Hon. Peter Paul Henderson,
  Founder,
  First Chairperson, and
  Chairperson Emeritus
Harold Gonzalez,
  Treasurer
Carol Archer
Louella Buckminster
George Colberg
Samuel Fales
Pat Greenlaw
Rev. Bryant Horsinger
George Horton
Bruce Knight
Harriet Lortz
Kathleen O'Reilly

Gladys Pepper
Alan Scala
Joseph Shapiro
Beth Trister
Vincent Wenski
Paul Widen
Felice Workenthrader
Cyrus Yarborough
Lucas Zukert

Staff:
Jack Neal, Executive
  Secretary
Paula Masonowitz,
  Office Manager
  Administrative
    Assistant,
  Assistant Secretary, and
  Assistant Treasurer

Preface

Volunteering should produce results and inspiration. It should also be fun.

In previous books such as _Effective Leadership in Voluntary Organizations_ and _America's Voluntary Spirit_, I've tried to share experiences and information that might contribute to increased performance and satisfaction. _The Board Member's Book_ tried to do some of both and added a third part called "Minutes of the Last Meeting," intended to provide a lighter moment. Out of those "Minutes" has grown this fuller glimpse of the hapless but humorous band who comprise Our Organization.

In poking fun at my own kind, I draw on 35 years of camaraderie and affection and an absolute conviction that along the way of service and dedication there should be fun.

Brian O'Connell
McLean, VA
July 24, 1987

OUR ORGANIZATION

Order of Records from the Official Minutes Book

1. Minutes of Our June Board Meeting
2. Minutes of Our September Board Meeting
3. Minutes of Our November Board Meeting
4. Minutes of Our January Board Meeting
5. Notes from Our Annual Meeting (Our Big Fifteenth) in February
6. Minutes of Our March Board Meeting
7. Notes from Our Board Retreat in April
8. Minutes of Our May Board Meeting

Minutes of Our June Board Meeting

Mr. Russell opened the meeting at 8:07 P.M. and immediately turned the meeting over to me, Mrs. Jeffrey (Effie) Black, Secretary of the Board of Directors, for reading of the minutes of the last meeting. I announced that copies would be distributed at the conclusion of the reading. Mr. Scala asked if they could be distributed immediately so that we might dispense with the reading. I pointed out to Mr. Scala—as I had on several previous occasions— that Robert's Rules of Order requires a reading of the minutes. I also indicated that I had gotten out of a sickbed to fulfill this duty.

Mr. Russell suggested that we compromise by distributing the minutes in advance but still proceeding with the reading, and everyone agreed. Mr. Scala, in a rare display of cooperation, complimented the Chairperson for having the diplomacy to propose what he called a "Read Along." He suggested that for our next meeting we

put the minutes to music and call it a "Minute's Minuet."
Everyone chuckled. Mrs. Lortz said that any composition
as long as my minutes couldn't be called a minuet.
Nobody laughed. I read the minutes.

The Chairperson next called on the Treasurer to give
the financial report. Mr. Gonzalez said that our income
for the first five months of this year was only $73,000, but
projected receipts for the second half of the year were
$809,000. Ms. Trister asked if this was realistic, but Mr.
Gonzalez pointed out that as Treasurer, he dealt with
expenses, not income. Ms. Trister apologized.

The Treasurer said he had heard indirectly that fundraising looked terrific. George Colberg asked if this was
reflected yet in the financial statements. Mr. Gonzalez
directed the question to our Executive Secretary, who
said that bookkeeping was a little behind because our
one-day-a-week bookkeeper/dictaphone-transcriber/ tele-
phone-operator and general handyperson had been on
maternity leave and had just delivered a little boy. Everyone clapped and agreed to a resolution to send a letter of
congratulations to the proud parents. A committee was
appointed to select a gift.

The bookkeeping situation prompted Mr. Colberg to
ask if we had an audit for last year. Jack apologized,
saying that we still don't, but adding that we have to be
patient because the service is being done for free by Mrs.
Workenthrader's brother, who used to be an accountant
but who is now in the Peace Corps and is away a lot.

Mr. Colberg asked whether Mr. Neal or Mr. Gonzalez
had any general idea of what the income looked like in
the half month since the May statement. Jack deferred to
the Treasurer, who said that as manager of the branch
where the association did its banking, he was aware that
deposits were dropping off and that the Executive Secretary had inquired what a line of credit was. Other than

2

that, he didn't know and would have to defer to the Fundraising Chairperson. Mr. Widen said he would prefer waiting to give his report until there was a more positive atmosphere.

Jack Neal said he didn't want to ignore some rough patches in our financial picture, but that he could confide to the Board that he had heard from an attorney in town that the association might be getting a nice bequest. In answer to questions, Jack said that he didn't know absolutely how much or how soon. This prompted Mrs. O'Reilly to ask if we knew whether the benefactor was dead yet. Jack said he had felt it was too delicate a question to ask. The Honorable Peter Paul Henderson, Founder, First Chairperson, and Chairperson Emeritus, said he would check around to see if he could find out who it was and, if the person were still alive, whether we could hope that events might still help our cash flow this year. Everyone expressed appreciation.

Mr. Gonzalez said that on the expense side, things looked much better, that we were only 16 percent above last year's figure. Mr. Knight said this was indeed good news, but didn't he recall that we had cut the budget by about 20 percent? The Treasurer acknowledged we had, but explained that just because a Board cuts the budget, this doesn't mean that expenses go down. There was a long, thoughtful silence.

Mrs. Archer said she didn't know much about finances, but was she close to the mark in guessing that, with income so far below expectations and expenses so far above budget, the picture was somewhat negative?

Mr. Colberg asked the Treasurer how he, from a banker's perspective, would assess the situation if income for the last half of the year was only as good as the first half, and if expenditures remained at their current level. Mr. Gonzalez, responding in the professional spirit in which the question was asked, replied, "Stinky." In terms of figures, he indicated that the shortfall would be about $475,000.00 against reserves of $19,875.53. Mrs. Masonowitz, the Assistant Treasurer, asked what a line of credit was. To put things on a more positive track, Mr. Russell asked the Fundraising Chairperson to report.

Mr. Widen explained that there were some disappointments. To begin with, the Special Event with a half-million-dollar goal fell short. We had not been able to get Bob Hope, Frank Sinatra, Jack Benny (Mr. Widen complained that staff had not told him that Benny was dead), or their backup, President Reagan, and we had to settle for Merty Pink, the first woman deejay at Station WOLP, who turned out to be less of a drawing card than was hoped. The event raised $783.87.

Expenses were $1,113.53. But Mr. Widen said, "We got great publicity for the association, so the overall effort should be viewed as a long-term investment."

The direct-mail solicitation also came up short. Mr. Widen and his advisers had assumed that with the emotional pull our cause represents, plus the power of this Board and the success of so many less worthy mail campaigns, we didn't need the ridiculous expense of a direct-mail firm or the loss of precious time in test marketing. Mr. Widen had volunteered to write the letters himself and to have them reproduced on his mimeograph. He reminded the Board that he had asked all of them to take a supply home and to mail them to all their friends. As of the meeting date, all of the returns were not in (thirteen of the twenty-four Board members had not yet mailed theirs), but, being realistic, this part of the campaign would have to be viewed as a failure. The costs so far, not including staff time, were $1,756, and income was $98, not including an "in-kind" gift by the Fundraising Chairperson's own company. This gift was valued at

$2,500 for reproduction, proofreading, messenger delivery, etc. Everyone thanked Mr. Widen for his personal generosity.

Actually, not everyone. Mrs. Buckminster asked Mr. Widen if the expenses included any reimbursements to his firm. Mr. Widen asked that the Chairperson rule the question as out of order, rude, and hurtful. Fortunately, Jack Neal volunteered the information that Mr. Widen had given a great party for the guys and gals in his shop and in the association, all of whom had done most of the work on the mail appeal. Mr. Neal said that this extra effort on behalf of the campaign added spirit and thrust to the Fundraising Drive and, therefore, was not only in good taste, but entirely within accounting standards. Besides, he pointed out, many of the hors d'oeuvres were donated.

Mr. Zukert asked what was the average contribution from the letters the Board members themselves had sent out. The answer was $3.26. There was extended discussion about whether this was the result of the Board members not having the right friends, not having enough friends, or, for the thirteen who had not mailed any letters, having no friends at all. After a heated exchange, it was agreed to refer the issue to the Nominating Committee.

Mr. Widen then reported on the part of the Drive involving contributions from the Board members themselves. He reminded the group that it was an axiom of Board membership that the Board exists to provide "wisdom, work, and wealth." The Honorable Peter Paul Henderson, Founder, First Chairperson, and Chairperson Emeritus, reacted, as he had on previous occasions, by saying that he found the phrase crass and undignified. Mr. Widen indicated that it was not necessary for Mr. Henderson to remind the Board of the value of his years of service involved in founding the association and guiding it to its current level.

The advance gifts solicitation from the Board was to have been the "leadership" part of the Drive, but was not yet underway. It has been the major subject of seven Board meetings. Most recently, the Board has not been able to agree on whether there should be a suggested level or standard for contributions from the Board. This issue, in turn, has been subdivided into two issues:

1. Should the time given by Board members be considered in lieu of cash?

Mr. Russell, our Chairperson, is on record as saying that ordinarily the dollar value of volunteer time should not be considered, but that in his case there should be an exception, particularly in light of how much time he is having to spend at the task. (It is assumed this would also apply to the demanding office of Secretary.)

2. Should "in-kind" gifts be considered?

Mrs. Archer has, on several occasions, reminded the group that while it was a pleasure to host the Board's Christmas party at her lovely home, it was still an expense which her husband's tax deduction hadn't begun to cover. Mr. Shapiro has told her that, on that basis, he hoped the flowers the Board sent for the party had been treated as income. The resulting exchange was ruled off the record, but it led to a suggestion that the Board clarify its legal liability coverage.

Mr. Russell gave his regular speech about harmony and the joy of working together in a great crusade. (Please see any previous minutes for exact wording.)

After a cooling-off break, Mr. Widen continued his report on fundraising. He said there had been a few other setbacks. The telethon had turned out to compete with an unexpected seventh game of the World Series. To compound the problem, it had been carried on a cable channel not yet hooked up in our town (but several people in Charles County had said it came through loud and clear). The net loss was $9,828.41. Though the Fundraising Chairperson described the total as a disappointment, he felt that the experience and exposure would stand the association in good stead. He also said we may want to consider expanding to Charles County to take advantage of the softening up already accomplished there.

The door-to-door campaign had run into a discouraging obstacle. Mr. Widen and his campaign advisers gave long and careful consideration to the choice of a time when the most people would be at home, and they had been fortunate to get a permit for a Sunday. Mr. Widen indicated, with some pride, that obviously no one else had been alert enough to come up with the idea. The only disappointing aspect was that the committee had never in this world believed that 95 percent of their volunteers would be so disloyal as to stay home on Super Bowl Sunday. The net loss was $13,870.

Mr. Widen summarized that, all in all, it hadn't been nearly as good a year as had been hoped. He said that perhaps in the remaining months they would be able to try some additional gimmicks. Mrs. Greenlaw said that she didn't think the association could afford any more fundraising.

Mrs. Lortz asked permission to bring up a timely matter and, with the Chairperson's assent, reintroduced her stale idea for an auxiliary. This time she emphasized the favorable fundraising role that other auxiliaries play for their organizations. With that comment, several Board members became rigidly alert. Mrs. Lortz said that there were certain ironclad rules necessary for the success of an auxiliary that, if followed, could result in thousands and, eventually, maybe millions of dollars for the association. She said that if this organization would provide the seed money to set up the auxiliary and would allow the auxiliary to be totally autonomous, she could guarantee results and might even be willing to head it herself. Mr. Gonzalez asked if the income of the auxiliary would go to the association, and the answer was decidedly affirmative—but only after the auxiliary's own projects were fully funded and endowed.

Mr. Colberg asked what the auxiliary would do. Mrs. Lortz responded that it would have its own bylaws, officers, board, bank accounts, and, as soon as possible, staff and office. "But what would it do?" Mr. Colberg persisted. Mrs. Lortz explained that until the auxiliary was established and its officers and board were in place, it would be inappropriate to speak for them.

The matter of an auxiliary was tabled.

Mr. Russell said it was time for committee reports.

In the absence of the Vice Chairperson, Mrs. Mitchell (who has missed three of the last five meetings, six of the last ten, and nineteen of thirty), Mr. Shapiro gave the report of the Personnel Committee.

The Board had referred to this committee the disagreement between the Executive Secretary and Mrs. Mitchell over who should approve sick leave. The Committee, recognizing that Mrs. Mitchell has had much more personnel experience than the Executive Secretary, recommended that all personnel decisions reside with her. Because of the sensitivity of the issue, the staff was asked to leave the room and the Board quickly approved the Committee report. (While in executive session, the Board also voted to move the office, give a raise to "great old Paula," and revise the letterhead.)

The Committee also reported its position on maternity leave. They said that because the current staff were all over forty, with the exception of Beverly, the one-day-a-week bookkeeper/dictaphone-transcriber/telephone-operator and general handyperson who had just had a baby, there was no need for a policy. The Board approved but said that should anyone get pregnant, the matter would be raised again. Mr. Zukert said that when the issue comes up again the idea of coverage for paternity should also be considered. Mrs. O'Reilly snapped that if a man is involved in paternity, the association has no obligation whatsoever, and the matter was dropped.

The next report was from the Bylaws Committee, with Ms. Trister reporting for Mr. Fales who was absent (due to personal circumstances—different from the personal circumstances that kept him from the last meeting).

The Committee presented its seventeenth draft of the proposed Bylaws revisions, which have now stretched over four and a half years of study. At the Board's last meeting, some had objected to the language of proposed amendments to Article XXCVI, Section 78c (Removal of Committee Members) because it might have been construed to provide a Committee Chairperson with arbitrary authority to dismiss members who were consistently in the minority.

The new revised proposal included a new phrase: "Consistent losers, no matter how often on the wrong side, are protected by due process." To underscore this point, the Committee added a parenthetical phrase: "(This sacred institution, under God, shall neither be ruled by the tyranny of the majority nor the tyranny of the minority.)"

That amendment, as revised, was officially moved and seconded. During discussion, it was pointed out that the use of the term "minority" could be misread, and, therefore, it was moved to add the word "numerical" in front of both "minority" and "majority" wherever they appeared. The motion to amend the revised amendment to the Bylaws was seconded.

Ms. Trister reminded the Board that the Bylaws Committee had spent two evenings crafting this revised language and that she was not sure she and Mr. Fales could hold the Committee together much longer if the Board continued to behave like a board of editors rather than a board of directors—and, on that basis, she flatly rejected any such amendment. Several members applauded.

Mr. Widen sympathized with the Bylaws Committee, but said that in the spirit of democracy, Bylaws should reflect the will of the governed. Several members clapped (including two who had already clapped on the other side). In this spirit, Mr. Widen offered an amendment to the amendment to the revised amendment to the Bylaws, which read, "Minorities reflected by numbers, race, ethnic origin, gender, sexual preference, or Christian denomination."

Mr. Zukert pointed out that not all religions are Christian and, therefore, he moved that in the amendment to the amendment to the revised amendment to the Bylaws, "Christian denomination" be stricken. Mrs. Lortz moved that in the parenthetical section, the phrase beginning, "This sacred institution, under God . . . ," be dropped because it flew in the face of separation of church and state. Mr. Widen agreed to accept her suggestion as part of his motion, but the seconder to Mr. Widen's motion did not, and, therefore, Mrs. Lortz asked that as a matter of principle she, as a Christian herself, be the one to move that the whole parenthetical clause be stricken from the record.

A howl of protest erupted. Rev. Horsinger offered a Solomon-like solution in the form of a substitute motion which proposed that in the amendment to the amendment to amend the revised Bylaws, instead of striking the words "Christian denomination," the word "religion" be substituted. Mrs. O'Reilly shouted that she sympathized wholly with Rev. Horsinger's intent, but that it left a loophole wide enough for the devil himself to drive through. She asked if he would accept an amendment to his substitute motion so that instead of just "religion" the phrase would be: "God-fearing religions, definitely not including some of the new weirdo cults." There was strong applause. Before Rev. Horsinger could reply, Mrs. Lortz was on her feet demanding that everybody was out of order until her motion of principle could be addressed.

To bring order to the chaos, the more experienced George Horton moved the previous question, but his intent was frustrated when Lucas Zukert asked which of the nine previous questions he was talking about. Pandemonium prevailed.

Finally, Mrs. Greenlaw, shouting above the others, demanded a point of personal privilege and, when recognized, said, "I move that I'm lost." Mr. Scala asked if he would accept an amendment to say: "We are all lost," and said authoritatively that Robert's Rules gave this motion the highest order. Mrs. Lortz challenged whether a motion that "We are all lost" had a higher standing than a motion of principle, and Mr. Horton assured her that it did.

Ms. Trister said that because this item was only the first of sixteen recommendations of the Bylaws Committee to be considered by the Board that evening, she hoped that the Board would be willing for her to take all of these ideas back to the Committee and to come forward at another meeting with a proposal incorporating all of the various motions and ideas. Mr. Widen said if they could do that, they could leave God in wherever they wanted.

The Chairperson said that unraveling all these motions would have to start with the person who made the last motion being willing to be the first to back off, so that the matter could be referred back to the Committee, and so forth down through each of the people who had made a motion. Mrs. O'Reilly said she would obstruct the process unless she was guaranteed that a Catholic would be added to the Bylaws Committee. In the interest of peace and sanity, Mr. Russell guaranteed that every person who had made a motion had a right to be certain that an individual of his or her political, philosophical, religious, or sexual preference would be represented on the Bylaws Committee. On that basis, the unraveling proceeded.

Ms. Trister announced that the second item the Bylaws Committee was to bring before the Board related to whether the organization should use the term Chairman, Chairwoman, Chairperson, or Chair. Before she could offer her first motion, Mr. Russell gave the Board its choice of a recess, adjournment, or dissolution, and fled the room.

On reconvening, the Chairperson said that in the interest of a change of pace, he was taking the privilege of moving ahead to the idea of having a "Board Retreat." Mr. Zukert kicked off the discussion about a one- or two-day retreat, when all the Board members would go off together to some secluded place to have a good block of uninterrupted time to really think about the state of the association and to get to know one another better. Mr. Knight was concerned that his wife would be terribly upset about his participating in such a co-ed venture. Mrs. Greenlaw said his wife had no idea how safe she was.

Mr. Shapiro wanted to know what exactly would be accomplished during a retreat. Mr. Zukert pointed out that all of the Board's regular meetings were so taken up with the kind of important matters we had been discussing that evening that there was never a chance to really "brainstorm" or engage in "blue skying." Mrs. Archer wanted to know how you got that kind of a process going, and Mr. Zukert indicated that most often it just starts with people talking off the tops of their heads. Mrs. Archer responded that this was not something this group needed to go away for two days to get good at.

Mr. Zukert asked the group to put aside immediate considerations and to try to see the idea from the point of view of the Board members getting to know one another's strengths and weaknesses. Mr. Gonzalez said that might be pressing our luck.

Ignoring these immediate doubts about the process, Mr. Zukert asked the group where such a session might be held. Four locations were suggested, but the reactions were so violently divided that Mr. Zukert concluded that a group which couldn't decide on the location for a retreat probably wasn't ready for one.

The final report for this meeting was by the Evaluation Committee and was presented by Mrs. Buckminster. She pointed out that the Committee deliberately included some "hard-nosed businessmen," as well as a number of social scientists and others who were used to "getting to the heart of the matter." She assured the Board that the language of the Committee was laced with such concrete terms as "bottom line," "cost effectiveness," and "management by objectives," and that this was one evaluation where just doing good was not good enough. For example, she said that one of the businessmen had been particularly helpful in pointing out that our program of public education would always defy quantitative analysis, and therefore we should drop any pursuits that can't be measured in specific body counts.

Rev. Horsinger interjected that it was wrong for a voluntary organization to sell its soul for the sake of doing something just because it can be measured. Mrs. Buckminster responded by asking the Reverend why he thought the Girl Scouts sell cookies?

Mr. Colberg said that if the churches had more doers and fewer worshippers, or more sales than prayers, there would be a more businesslike approach to God, and a lot more souls could be saved per minister. The Reverend seemed moved by this admonition and asked how the idea might be implemented. Mr. Colberg said he couldn't be specific, but there was no doubt in his mind that all churches and other nonprofit organizations, with all their bleeding-heart do-gooders, would be much better off if the people working in them had M.B.A. degrees rather than their abstract training in divinity, archeology, social work, or library science. He capped his point by asking, "How many Bibles has theology ever sold?"

Mr. Russell asked what this hard-nosed Committee had concluded, and Mrs. Buckminster said that the findings of their two-year evaluation could be summarized as follows: "Any organization made up of such bright people, who are so dedicated and who have worked so hard, must be doing a great deal of good."

Some Board members wept.

On that positive note, the meeting was adjourned at 11:16 P.M.

Respectfully submitted,

Mrs. Jeffrey (Effie) Black
Secretary of the Board of Directors

Minutes of Our September Board Meeting

Mr. Russell began the meeting at 8:13 P.M. (though he had tried to start it at 8:04 and again at 8:10). He said that "after the long summer break, maybe we should take turns and introduce ourselves and say where we're from." Everybody chuckled.

By prior agreement, negotiated among the officers over the summer, it had been arranged that minutes of meetings would be sent in advance, but that the Secretary would present highlights before the floor was opened for comments and approval.

Only a quarter of an hour into my highlights, Mrs. Lortz interrupted with, "It would be less painful to go back to reading the blessed things!" I stuck to my side of the bargain. Indeed, I found that freed from the actual text I could improvise with a bit of what my mother always said was my natural storytelling ability.

Mr. Gonzalez was not so fortunate. What started as a

rehash of June's searing review took a surprising turn when Mrs. Archer switched the discussion to the terminology of the financial reports. She indicated, for example, that in July and August she had taken an "I'm OK—You're OK" course, which taught her that people shouldn't always start with negative thoughts. On that basis, she wondered why we couldn't make a point of beginning these discussions by looking at a piece of paper that just showed our income and assets without reference to any liabilities. Mr. Colberg responded that she was setting a trap for herself, because what he was looking at in terms of income and assets was "not OK," and the liabilities were certainly "not OK," so one way or another we were going to get depressed.

Undeterred, Mrs. Archer said that maybe the problem would be eased if we stopped calling them liabilities. She pointed out that in the rehabilitation field the professionals had learned long ago that any terms like "crippled" or "handicapped" or "disabled" just call attention to the negative, and they had learned to call such things "abilities" and "opportunities" and "strengths." Warming to her topic—and encouraged by the strong nods of Mr. Gonzalez and Jack Neal, who were pleased with any excuse to avoid the figures—she expanded on her ideas and said that all of our meetings get started on a negative note with our oppressive financial reports and that it would have a liberating effect, which might turn the association completely around if we could find a way to emphasize the good news in our figures. It was clear that much of the Board agreed, but no one seemed to be able to come up with ways to do it.

Caught up in the spirit of this, Gladys Pepper suggested that we might use our problems to advantage if we would treat them as a spur to overcome our liabilities. Mr. Yarborough picked up the metaphor, but not the mood, when he held up the reports and responded, "If we want to look at it that way, I think our little junkie just hit bottom."

The discussion then zeroed in on whether it was best psychologically to present the reports early in the meeting, as a goad to progress, or to postpone them to the end of the meeting, where they wouldn't interfere with the good temper of the Board. After lengthy discussion, during which several members suggested that the reports be presented at about the middle of the meetings, it was agreed to appoint a committee to study the format, terminology, and psychological significance of our financial presentations. Mr. Colberg suggested that the proposed committee look also at content, but by then the Board had spent itself on the financial issues and was ready to move on.

At this point in the meeting, Mr. Wenski arrived and apologized for his tardiness. He explained that he had come home early to be sure to have ample time to get ready to be on time but started out watching the evening news at 5:30 and ended up watching two sets of local news, Dan Rather, and McNeil-Lehrer, and by then he was so depressed he just couldn't get going. Mrs. Buckminster welcomed him to the 8:00 news.

Mr. Zukert said that whatever was decided about the financial reports he hoped that they, along with the minutes and other materials, could be sent to the Board at least a week before the meetings. He said it was hard to deal with some of the issues without advance study. Jack Neal explained that this matter had come up often before, but, as he explained each time, his office doesn't get some necessary information until the last minute, and the crew doesn't really get geared up for a meeting until a day or even the evening before, so if they had to get everything out a week in advance, the meetings would have to be held a week later.

There was an unusually long pause, during which some people looked around for affirmation of the simple logic of this, and others sought the opposite. Mr. Zukert started to sort it out but decided that somehow there had to be more to Jack's reasoning than appeared anywhere near the surface, and he thought it only fair to himself and to Jack to think about it before expressing a reaction.

The Chairperson, sensing that this was not the moment for objectivity, announced that he was taking the liberty of postponing the Board's scheduled session for evaluation of the Executive Secretary. (Mr. Zukert probably thought to himself that if he was right about the prior issue, they ought not to postpone the evaluation too long.)

On the general subject of materials for the Board, Ms. Trister, a new Board member, asked if the Board could also get minutes of Executive Committee meetings. A collective gasp filled the room. Paula Masonowitz, Office Manager, Administrative Assistant, Assistant Secretary, Assistant Treasurer, and oldest employee of the association, went pale at the thought of what would happen next. Fortunately, and as further indication of why he is our leader, Mr. Russell was the first to recover, and while the others were too numb to react, he moved swiftly to gain control of the situation. He decided this request could only be dealt with in the association's tradition of minimum candor.

In measured tones, Mr. Russell explained that because the Executive Committee deals with so many sensitive matters, its meetings have to be off the record. He apologized but said that as experienced volunteers he was sure that Ms. Trister and the rest of the Board would understand. He indicated that the Executive Committee had met eleven times since the last Board meeting and had worked very hard on behalf of the Board. Mrs. Archer asked if he could give some examples of what they had been doing, but Mr. Russell could only say that they had been dealing with across-the-board issues which had saved the Board countless time and upset. He would say that they covered such explosive and grisly topics as annual meeting speakers, approval of expense reports, reconciling of petty cash (including forgiveness of shortages!), approval of public positions and statements, disputes between the Chairperson and Executive Secretary, and many other crucial questions. Mrs. O'Reilly asked, "What the hell are *we* for?" In the same patient way, Mr. Russell explained that "the Board is like a joint session of Congress, the Supreme Court, and the ultimate authority on all matters all rolled into one." The enormity of this example took the ardor out of what was the closest we would ever come to mutiny.

As feelings subsided, but before they were quieted, Mr. Widen asked, "If the Board doesn't know what's going on, how can it exercise ultimate authority?" The Honorable Peter Paul Henderson, Founder, First Chairperson and Chairperson Emeritus, realizing that this was a moment for statesmanship, got to his feet and, once steadied, intoned, "The Executive Committee is there to handle all the really thoughtful and controversial matters which a large, unwieldy, and generally uninformed Board could never address with knowledge, experience, and time, but the bylaws and common practice call for there to be a Board, so that's why we have both."

Spent of wisdom and energy, our senior leader folded back into his chair. (In that instant it must have crossed Mr. Zukert's mind that maybe the evaluation should include Founder Henderson too.)

Mr. Scala asked if it was all right to know who is on the Executive Committee, and at least seven people shifted uneasily. Tiring of this continuing challenge, Mr. Russell responded somewhat testily that for the good of the individuals and the organization, and really for the good of every Board member, "the Executive Committee list is secret and will remain so." He returned to a more politic posture by adding that many of its members were present at the table at that very moment. An electric tingle vibrated through the room.

Mrs. Buckminster asked if, among the sensitive matters discussed and settled routinely by the Executive Committee, the Executive Secretary's salary had come up. Jack Neal slumped in a contortion of pain and fright. Mr. Russell said that he would not be revealing a confidence to say that this year they had done so, though usually the matter was referred to the even smaller Personnel Committee so that the fewest possible number would know. Mrs. Buckminster probed to learn what the salary was, and by now several others had joined Jack in body language that indicated horror and cramps. Sensing some small victory, several Board members pressed to gain at least an impression of the general salary range. To establish some sense of cooperation, Mr. Russell said that he could not answer the question directly, but he would give the Board three guesses.

"Under $100,000?" asked Archer.

"Yes," said Russell.

"Thank God," said Colberg.

"Does the figure we're talking about include benefits?" asked Zukert.

"Yes," said Russell, but added, "That's question two."

"Foul!" cried Zukert.

"Is it between $20,000 and $50,000?" asked Knight.

"Generally," said Russell.

And just before discussion was closed, Greenlaw queried, "Next time can we play twenty questions?"

The next matter involved selecting delegates for the state convention. Paula explained that ordinarily we would have five delegates, but because we are behind in our dues again, we only get two and a half delegates and two and a half alternates. George Horton wanted to know how in the world you could have a half delegate but Felice Workenthrader replied, "All you need to do is attend one of those sessions and you'll know." Despite this characterization, competition for the available slots was intense. Before the sparring got unpleasant, we had to work our way through the formula of a half delegate, which produced a number of remarks that were intended to be humorous but which bordered on profane. Officials at the state office punished us more than they thought when they reduced us to a half delegate.

It was Harriet Lortz who finally suggested the solution of having the same person serve as both the half delegate and the half alternate. We were all so relieved that there was clapping and a cacophony of "Here, here." Alan Scala exclaimed, "With that kind of mind, maybe we've got ourselves a *real* Treasurer," and then, catching himself, he turned to a pained Mr. Gonzalez and said, "Just kidding, Harry." But the awkwardness around the table communicated a shared thought that maybe a new Treasurer was what we needed to make the figures better.

When the choosing got serious, it was obvious that, as always, Mr. Henderson had to be asked to lead the delegation. Only Chairperson Russell had the courage and quick-mindedness to suggest that our Founder could actually attend as an at-large delegate. Jack Neal coughed nervously, pointing out that while that was so, our budget did not cover expenses for at-large delegates.

This led Mr. Shapiro to ask what reimbursement we provided, and that led to a new discussion. We give seven cents a mile and thirty-five dollars per diem. After long and fruitless discussion, we acknowledged that, while these fees are not altogether realistic, it is far more than we can afford. During the discussion, it was even suggested that we might ask the delegates to pick up their total expenses. Mr. Henderson's look of horror killed that idea.

Louella Buckminster said the expenses were eased somewhat if people doubled up in rooms, but Mrs. O'Reilly wanted to know what happens if there isn't an even number of women. Rev. Horsinger raised his eyebrows, but Mr. Russell assured him that it was not that kind of convention. Under his breath, Alan Scala was heard to whisper, "The odd person gets Henderson."

Mr. Russell said that, because of a business conflict, he would not be able to go. Someone who wasn't thinking said that it would be logical for Penelope Mitchell to be next in line because she is our Vice Chairperson. It was left to me to point out that Mrs. Mitchell has missed four of the last six meetings, seven of the last ten, and twenty of the last thirty. Rev. Horsinger, in foolish fairness, said that was a matter which the Nominating Committee should resolve and that as long as she is our Vice Chairperson she should have the chance. Because he had put it on such a high moral basis, no one wanted to take him on.

On the heels of this contention, the Board, with soothing unanimity, selected the Secretary for the other delegate's spot. My acceptance speech was warmly received.

It followed that Mr. Gonzalez, as Treasurer, should be selected as our half delegate/half alternate. Then, having covered the officers, the choices for alternates were particularly difficult. At one point, it came down to figuring the balance of men and women, and in an effort to give Mr. Gonzalez some choice in the matter, Ms. Trister asked

Harry who he would want to sleep with. It was hard to know who was the more embarrassed.

Someone suggested that Harry Gonzalez and Jack Neal could sleep together and that seemed to settle it, until someone remembered that Paula is Jack Neal's staff alternate.

Vincent Wenski, who obviously wasn't at the last Board meeting and didn't read the minutes, said that he thought we should offer a chance to Paul Widen as a reward for his fundraising. It would be an extreme understatement to say that the suggestion was greeted with coolness. For sixty seconds, no one moved their eyes from the ceiling molding. Sensing that the wind was not likely to shift in his direction, Mr. Widen said that he just remembered he was going to have to attend a funeral that weekend anyway.

During the prolonged silence, it had become obvious that Founder Henderson was finding every conceivable way to make displeasure apparent, and it was then that we remembered we had not resolved the question of his role and expenses. At some risk, I suggested that he should take my place or Penelope Mitchell's, who had been absent so much anyway. The dilemma was solved when Mr. Shapiro suggested that the budget was already shot anyway, so we might as well pay Mr. Henderson's expenses as a delegate-at-large. Mr. Gonzalez came up with the unique idea of having Mrs. Henderson serve as one of our alternates, which would solve the problem of who Mr. Henderson would sleep with.

It was agreed that the final alternate's spot could not be decided until we knew who might not be going, what sex they were, who would still be available, who might be willing to pay their own way, and who would be available after all the above factors had been decided. With our earlier criteria in mind, Mr. Colberg said—*and please note that I am quoting*—"that any rich, bisexual halfass would do." Almost everybody laughed. Mrs. Archer asked to be recorded as not laughing. Mrs. O'Reilly, who had actually laughed, said that she should be recorded that way too. And as a courtesy, I've put Rev. Horsinger in that column, though I think I caught him smiling.

With the delegation pretty much decided, we moved on to the subject of our own annual meeting.

Mr. Fales, who had been excused from the last two meetings for two different but equally forgivable reasons, reported on initial preparations for the February "Big One," our fifteenth Annual Meeting. He said his committee was close to recommending people for awards, but couldn't report on this until the next meeting. Mrs. Buckminster commented that after our marathon session on state convention delegates, we might not be ready for such discussions even by November.

The Board, as usual, did not involve itself with arrangements, but we were able to make some decisions on location, menu, price, parking arrangements, head table, ingredients for soft and hard punch, table decorations, name cards, table assignments, receiving line, guest list, photographer, location of registration table, and tipping. At our November and January meetings, when the event is closer, we will cover particulars. Details will be left to the committee and staff.

After a break, since it was getting late, we turned to the two major items of business, the question of whether to explore membership in the United Way, and our Program Committee's report.

After our last fundraising report, several Board members had suggested that there must be an easier way, which is how the subject of United Way got on our agenda.

Mr. Widen, Chairperson of this year's Fundraising

Drive, inadvertently gave us our starting place for discussion when he said that to go in now would be to admit failure.

Right on the heels of that, Mr. Gonzalez contributed another unintended push when he warned us that going in could dry up all our other sources of funds. If a vote had been taken after those two arguments against joining, the vote would have been unanimous—for signing on.

Mr. Yarborough said that we need to be prepared, that the United Way would expect all Board members of a participating agency to contribute their fair share. Ms. Trister confirmed, from experience with another board, that the United Way solicitation is so thorough that they actually study the giving records of agency trustees. On the basis of this important intelligence, the balance of sentiment careened to the other side.

For a while the spiral was downward. Of particular note was the experience that several Board members had with the allocations process. They reported that in representing other causes they had run into the horror of annual reporting requirements, hearings, reviews, and worse for every year's allotment. Mrs. Lortz said that the kinds of questions asked were:

How many people did you help?
How much did you help them?
What did it cost per limb or organ helped?
If you are involved with mental health, how much better are they in terms of—

Feeling good?
Happiness?
Fulfillment?
Euphoria?

Give approximate dollar cost per unit of feeling good, happiness, etc.

List qualifications of your staff.
List qualifications of your Board.

Mrs. Lortz said these were just a few that she could remember but that she would get one of the seventy-two-page forms and send it over to Jack Neal. It was close to 11:00 P.M. when we finished the litany of horror stories about United Way participation. The low point in the discussion came when Mr. Knight reported that he had once been with an agency that went into the United Way and never came out!

Slowly the tide began to shift back. It actually started when Mr. Shapiro was arguing against joining because he said they would always be looking over our shoulder and telling us what to do.

Somehow that caused a few of the Board members to realize that if we had to tell them what we do, we might have to figure it out for ourselves and maybe that wasn't all bad. Mr. Zukert mused that "maybe it would be a good way to get some training for Jack Neal or help in finding a new exec—if we ever needed it." Most everybody nodded agreement, until we realized that the only quiet head, filled with hurt, scared eyes, belonged to the object of our consideration.

By 11:30 P.M. the pendulum had swung back toward such favorable consideration that our attention had shifted to whether United Way would take us in. There was general agreement that with our visibility and record it would be a cinch, and that we should begin thinking primarily about our financial demands and other conditions.

We even seemed to get over the hurdle presented by

Mr. Scala, who reminded us that the United Way had recently done a community-wide "needs assessment" which had resulted in the establishment of twenty-three categories, rated in order of priority. While we didn't actually see ourselves in any of the categories, there was good reason to believe that we at least fell in between several of them.

After further discussion, it was agreed to "send out a search party," and we all raised our arms in a symbolic motion of "charge."

Unfortunately with the hour as late as it was, the report of the Program Committee had to be postponed, again.

Our Chairperson reminded everybody that at our next meeting we will have a guest from the National Office, who will tell us how we are doing compared to other chapters around the country.

The meeting was adjourned at 11:42 P.M.

Respectfully submitted,

Mrs. Jeffrey (Effie) Black
Secretary of the Board of Directors

Minutes of Our November Board Meeting

Mr. Russell opened the meeting at 8:35 P.M., after we had punch and cookies to meet and welcome our National Office representative, Geneva Betts, who was seated on his left. He also pointed out that our Vice Chairman, Penelope Mitchell, who sat at his right, was able to be with us after a few absences (three of six, seven of eleven, and twenty of thirty-one!). I said that the minutes would record that the new members and even several of the old ones were pleased to know what she looked like. Mrs. Mitchell said it was a shame that such sarcasm was wasted on a readership of one.

I was about to disprove her point when, to my horror and humiliation, the Chairperson suggested that out of deference to Ms. Betts, and to be sure we provided enough time to profit from her message, we depart from our standard format and postpone the minutes and financial report until later in the meeting. I started to point out that at the very least not starting with the minutes was highly irregular and more likely in violation of state law and the Constitution, but Mr. Shapiro outshouted me with his demand to know if we were going to downplay and ignore those "blood red numbers in the Treasurer's report?" Mr. Russell ground his teeth into a smile and said that perhaps we might wait until our guest left to discuss personal matters.

Ms. Betts said it was all right because we should treat her as part of the family. Treasurer Gonzalez, sensing his reprieve threatened, and speaking in the vernacular of family, told her to shut up and get up. Our Chairperson provided a more gracious introduction.

Geneva began by reminding us that she, too, had once been at the chapter level—in a state not far away—so she wanted us to think of her as the friendly big sister who, though she had gone on to National, still has empathy and sympathy for the local level. Penelope held a tissue to her eyes to keep from weeping, and Jack Neal held a handkerchief to his mouth to keep from gagging.

With one wary eye on Jack, Geneva said she liked to begin these reports with comments about all the positive things that the chapter is doing. There was a pained silence while she scanned her notes. Fixing on the one highlight she found recorded, she asked with the most upbeat tone she could muster, "I wonder how many of you realize that you are the only chapter in the country that has had its affiliation extended three times even though you've never met national standards?" We beamed at this honor.

Turning to other positives, Geneva told about the astounding growth rate of our nationwide crusade:

National income grew last year by 17 percent.
Membership grew by 22 percent.

Contributed radio and TV time was estimated by the broadcasting industry to be worth $506 billion.
Fifty-seven new local chapters were formed, bringing the new total to just under one thousand. And, six new states have been organized, bringing the total to fifty-nine.

With each announcement, the Honorable Peter Paul Henderson, our Founder, First Chairperson, and Chairperson Emeritus, slumped deeper into his chair, until his eyes were barely level with the table.

Then there was a litany of success stories about other chapters, filled with doubling or quintupling income, membership growth, surges of publicity, program impact, and on and on. One of our new Board members made the mistake of asking how we compared. Geneva reacted like a supervisor in an employee evaluation who has just begun trying to soften the blow before putting the person on probation, when the employee asks, "What about my raise?" With aplomb Geneva recovered, and taking advantage of the opening—albeit premature—said, "It's curious you should bring that up." She began with comparisons, moved to contrasts, and then slid into the vernacular of day and night. In fairness, she did it with candor, grace, and even humor, though some of her "good news—bad news" stories left us little doubt which side we were on.

At one point, for purposes of encouragement, she compared us with the Adams County unit—her one big mistake of the evening. She evidently pierced deep into the competitive instincts of our otherwise implacable leader, who for a moment lost his aplomb and, jumping to his feet, shook his finger at poor Ms. Betts and wailed, "Sure, and it's headed by old Ms. Richbitch Gotrocks who pours in money and gets all of her friends to do the same, and then they have charity balls and get their pictures all over the paper—and . . ." Catching himself, he apologized and sat down. Geneva got the point.

Ms. Betts was a bit more judicious in the selection of her second comparison, but when she described the particular chapter it was obvious that the secret of its success was that it had a highly qualified board, which caused George Colberg to comment, "Oh, that explains it." In frustration, Bruce Knight said that these examples weren't fair because they involved exceptional people, and Geneva should understand that, with no apologies, we accept ourselves as average. Warming to the point and wishing to put ourselves in better light for fairer comparison, Mr. Widen said, "We're even below average." There was a silence ripe with ambivalence. It is to Ms. Betts's distinct credit that she didn't take advantage of the opening.

Her third selection was more appropriate. At least it was further away. She outlined the work of the Washington County chapter in Maryland and said that we might model ourselves after them. She said she'd even taken the liberty of suggesting to the Maryland group that they enter into a "mentor" relationship with our chapter, and they were willing. To her disappointment, this didn't go over too well on our side. Mr. Yarborough said that the last time he had a tutor he flunked the subject, and, besides, her breath smelled. Mrs. Archer, who is heading our exploratory committee with United Way, said we were already having enough trouble trying to explain ourselves to outsiders, who seem to begin the relationship with an assumption that we are idiots. Mr. Horton said that he bet the Washington chapter got so good by going around stealing other people's secrets. In the only time that evening that she blew her cool, Ms. Betts retorted, "Coming here would be rather barren foraging."

While on the attack, she took up the matter of the

sloppiness, casualness, and even flippancy of our required reports to National. For example, she held up the thirty-nine page program report form for last year, on which the only thing written was "If and when our Board ever gets off its duff and does something, we'll have something to report." All eyes glared at Jack, who twisted grotesquely as he retched his way to the men's room.

It was finally obvious that our Executive Secretary was not going to return right away, so the meeting proceeded without him. Ms. Betts reported on the recent National annual meeting.

There had been several controversial resolutions which occupied hundreds of hours of debate. The major one, still totally unresolved, had proposed that all the units of the organization adopt a common name. This had come up two years ago, and a study had been called which showed that out of more than 500 chapters responding to the survey, there were 428 different names. There were groups, colonies, assemblies, congregations, bands, troupes, troops, centers, federations, caucusses, conferences, clans, in groups, out groups, conventicles, festivals, movements, fraternities, meeting grounds, and one that just refers to itself as "our organization."

There were two parts to the proposed resolution. The first called for agreement that there should be a common name, and this passed within minutes. The second proposed one of three suggested names, and after 490 proposed substitutions the study committee was extended for another two years.

Another resolution had also sought commonality and unity. It called for having one clear-cut national program priority for the whole organization. It was pointed out that if we did this, the whole organization would be moving in lock step, which was the secret of all great national crusades. Here, too, everyone agreed with the purpose and everyone disagreed on what the number one priority should be. In this case, though, a compromise resolution was accepted: "We, the Delegate Assembly, speaking with one unified national voice, hereby vote that each chapter, consistent with local circumstances, finances, customs, and idiosyncrasies, *must* give at least some thought to paying some attention to one or more of the forty-three program emphases adopted as first priority by this body."

Geneva said that the only resolution that took even more time than those two involved trying to agree on a change of fiscal year. With our year-end financial figures in mind, Mr. Colberg asked if the resolution included the possibility of having more than twelve months in a fiscal year. Unfortunately, it does not, but our National representative said that the resolution had been tabled, and that when it came up again she would propose this as a forty-seventh amendment.

There was one resolution that some of us thought pretty silly. There evidently was a proposal to have five National Vice Presidents rather than three, with each identified as first, second, third, and so forth. Mr. Fales said this was a waste of time and in any case, who in the world would want to be known as the "Fifth Vice President"? Mrs. Mitchell leaned over and, smiling at Geneva, said, "Each of us should be prepared to do whatever is necessary to help the organization."

One resolution got a predictable response. It proposed that the Delegate Assembly and the National Board, now approximately 85 percent male, should be required to have closer to a 50-50 balance. It was defeated by approximately 85 percent of the votes. Ms. Betts said it would be brought up again next year.

There is one particularly exciting new national development. National is undertaking a "bequest cultivation program" to increase the practice of leaving money to the organization in wills. They are really going at it in a major way and all of us are being asked to climb on board.

There had been a national competition, involving some of the best advertising agencies, to name the effort and, with considerable national fanfare, the winner had been announced at the annual meeting. The bequest program will be called "Give As You Go."

The runners-up had been

Expire Inspired
Make Your Last Breath Last
God Can Count.

There was a lot of support for the last one but many felt it was too subtle.

Some of the message will be included in the TV spot, which will show an aging actor looking hard into the camera and delivering this grabber:

God loves a cheerful giver,
and God loves the poor;
so approach the Judgment Day doubly blessed.

Mrs. Workenthrader said the only thing that would make it even better would be if after saying those words, the aged actor dropped dead.

In a rare display of unanimity, the Board voted to adopt the project.

On that happy note, the group gave Geneva a round of applause, and with that we broke to finish the punch and cookies.

When we resumed, Mr. Russell noted that Mr. Wenski had joined us. He apologized for being tardy, saying that he had to be with a woman whose husband had been kidnapped, leaving her distraught. Mrs. O'Reilly observed that it obviously wasn't his own wife, and the meeting returned to its normal tension.

I suggested that this would be a good time for the minutes but the Chairperson rushed on. Mr. Scala, thinking he was being funny, said that maybe I could mouth them while we were hearing other reports, and Penelope Mitchell chimed in, "That would indeed be a minimal subliminal." I decided to bide my time.

There was a report on awards from Mr. Fales of the Annual Meeting Committee.

He passed around a list of those who will be honored, including twenty-six groups and thirty-three individuals. Most of the discussion that followed could be compressed to "Why, Why, Why?" or, more fully, "Why this one? Why that one?" Mrs. O'Reilly summarized the sentiment of the Board: "There is hardly a damn one of them who has lifted a finger." Mr. Fales reminded the group with patience and pedantry that "awards are either for getting people out of an organization or for sucking them in." That stopped most of us.

Rev. Horsinger, with his usual naiveté, asked why all the newspapers and radio and TV stations were getting awards again this year when they hadn't yet given us any coverage. Picking up Mr. Fales's tone, Pat Greenlaw, speaking for the PR Committee, said, "If we don't honor them, they never will."

Ms. Trister noted that we were giving awards to all the volunteers who had given more than fifty hours and, with demure innocence, asked if that included Board members. Mr. Fales explained that the awards were reserved for volunteers. Beth looked quizzical but didn't press the point. (She told me later that in a future meeting she wanted to bring up the distinction between volunteers and Board members and even between Board members and staff, but I told her she was heading into very deep water.) Mrs. Lortz thought it was great that we were honoring these volunteers but felt it was a bad signal to be spending money on them. She thought that might interfere with the image of them as volunteers. Others said that it's the only thing we can give them to show our appreciation for all the free time they donate. It was agreed to go ahead with the awards but to not spend more than two dollars apiece. Mr. Horton snorted that with all the volunteers he had seen around, this might add up to four dollars.

Reflecting the good vibes at the close of Geneva Betts's report, and for other reasons not appropriate for minutes but which probably are obvious anyway, Mrs. Mitchell suggested that it would be a novel idea for us to give an award to the National Office. After all, she said, "They're always giving awards to chapters for best this and that, so why don't we turn it around and give them something?" Mr. Gonzalez said that from the mail he's been seeing, they would rather have money. Mrs. Pepper asked what we would honor them for, and several chimed in that we could express appreciation for the new bequest program. Mr. Colberg thought it would be better to wait and see how it pans out. We reluctantly agreed. There was a silence while we brainstormed how this award idea might be implemented. You could almost hear the buzz of minds at work.

After several minutes with not a single idea produced, Mr. Zukert offered, "We could give it to them for courage in keeping us affiliated." A committee was appointed to continue the brainstorming.

As always seems to happen, the Board spent what seemed like half the meeting talking about publicity for the Annual Meeting, and as usual there was a tug of war between Pat Greenlaw of the Public Relations Committee and Sam Fales of the Annual Meeting Committee as to who should lead this part of the discussion. The two did agree that if the Governor comes, much of the publicity will be handled by his staff, and our Chairperson tried, quite unsuccessfully, to leave the matter at that.

Mr. Wenski said that with all the media there to get their awards, publicity would pretty much take care of itself, but all of us recall the low point of last year's meeting when name after name was called, and the only award acceptance was by a woman whose son had once been a copy boy down at the News. Some of the weeklies do cover the story, but never mention much about the meeting or even the other award winners. They generally make it sound as though they had been singled out for a Pulitzer, but it's to their advantage not to make too much of the sponsor.

Pat Greenlaw complained that she couldn't be expected to get publicity if the association didn't generate interesting activities. Sam Fales countered that it was his understanding that good flacks have a nose for publicity and can generate it out of everyday happenings. Greenlaw countered, "It would make my day if one of your annual meetings could at least be ordinary—they're so damn dull that if Dan Rather attended he'd have to call off the next day's evening news." By this time, a number of Board members were stirred up and were clamoring for that one good idea that would make this year's meeting a colossal media event. The closest we came was when Mr. Knight suggested that we might switch the meeting to a nursing home and kick off the bequest program right then and there. Jack Neal, who had snuck back into the meeting by this time, said that we might even be lucky enough that one of the residents might pass away that very night and the headline the following day could be "A Kickoff Kickoff."

Pat Greenlaw, who didn't buy it and was somewhat defeated with this additional evidence of our less-than-successful blue skying, simply asked that we let her know if any ideas flashed through anyone's mind. Ever devoted to word association, Alan Scala, who was getting even more tired than the rest of us, giggled, "Wouldn't it be big news if the Mayor brought greetings and then shot the group with a flash and ran out?" Pat Greenlaw, who was so desperate for ideas that she found herself taking it seriously, said that she had heard that the Mayor had been known to do that in small groups and, with her mind racing, thought out loud, "If we could just get him to open up in this larger setting, we'd probably even make national TV." Mrs. O'Reilly reacted with horror, "It's bad enough to do it in a small group, and it's disgusting to do in large ones, and now you want him to do it on the Today Show!"

For the tenth year in a row, our long Board discussion of Annual Meeting publicity had aimed high—and crashed.

Mr. Russell asked Mrs. Greenlaw if she was ready to give the rest of the Public Relations Committee report and she said she wouldn't dare.

Jack Neal said that he needed to get authorization for the new Annual Report. Rev. Horsinger commented politely that he didn't recall having seen one for last year. Immediately, Jack knew he had made a mistake. But he was too far into it to back out, so he blundered ahead: "We haven't finished the financials or the artwork, and the advertising agency that agreed to do the copy and layout on a volunteer basis got lucky and has some paid work, and the Ajax Company hasn't given us an answer yet as to whether they will print it when they've got some down time on their press, but other than that it's due out any day." Mrs. Pepper asked if it were reasonable to ask why we need a new one if we don't have an old one, and Jack explained it was a new year, which Mrs. Pepper already knew. Neither quite knew what to say next.

Fortunately, Harriet Lortz moved the discussion ahead by suggesting that in the future we ought to have a lot more pictures, including shots of the Board in action. Mr. Colberg thought that might be hard to do. Mrs. Lortz persisted by saying that we all might take greater pride in the report and participate more fully in its distribution if the Directors were prominently featured in it. Mr. Colberg relented slightly, on the grounds that "it might at least spruce up our Board meetings." Mrs. O'Reilly said, "He should talk." She said people dressed better for Mass on a summer Sunday in Atlantic City than he ever did for a Board meeting. Then she grabbed him by the chin and, mimicking the advertisement, sang out, "Ring around the collar, ring around the collar."

Mr. Russell suggested that we stay away from further comments on one another's persons, but Mrs. O'Reilly interjected that it was the only fun she got out of Board meetings anymore.

Mr. Wenski said he hoped that whenever we do another Annual Report that at least we attempt to be different. He said that everybody's reports looked the same, and he made his point by asking us, "When was the last time we saw a nonprofit organization's Annual Report that didn't start with the Chairman's Report and then the Executive Secretary's Report? And we compound the problem by going one step worse and having a Founding Chairperson's Report that includes what must have been his high-school graduation picture." Poor Mr. Henderson was obviously not ready for the blow. He was at first surprised—then hurt, then distressed—and then he threw up his punch and cookies.

While several people rushed to his aid, young Beth

Trister sat stunned. "I've never seen someone literally toss their cookies before," she said.

All this put a damper on further discussion about creative aspects of the Annual Report. Besides, someone figured that we have missed three years already and that if we wait another two we could do a five-year wrap-up. Mrs. Buckminster said she thought that made sense and that by then we may have enough to fill it up; to which Mr. Shapiro added, "And maybe a financial report that won't send us to jail."

Mr. Widen responded for the team that had been chosen to make an exploratory visit to some of the foundations in town. Their initial visit had been to the Cutting Edge and Fail Safe Foundation (CEFS). They learned that for the exploratory session, at least with CEFS, you don't actually see a person. At this stage it's entirely automated. As Mr. Widen explained it, "In the lobby there is a machine which is activated when you open the door. It provides a history of the foundation, including the founder's early years, courtship days, background on how he made so very much money—mostly brilliance, persistence, clean living, and a partnership with his wife, who didn't seem to be the same woman he had courted—and the donor's philosophy of philanthropy: 'We give only to those who are very needy, aggressive, bright, self-starters who can pull themselves up by their bootstraps.' The words and the voice discourage anyone who doesn't qualify from going the next step. Our team found itself wondering how many people fit those criteria and are still very poor and we guessed that's why the foundation has so much money.

"We decided that as long as we were there we might as well proceed, so we punched the obviously hardly-ever-used button number two. This produced a printout of the foundation's fields of interest, which was followed by a running listing of the things CEFS doesn't fund. There was so much to absorb in both these sections that when it was over we punched number two again and tried to make notes from as much of the fifteen-minute presentation as possible.

"As nearly as my records can tell, the foundation is only interested in local projects, the closer to the neighborhood the better, that have the best chance of protecting the ozone layer.

"That was pretty straightforward, but the don'ts were harder to keep track of. They have one of those annual medical-exam forms that ask you if you have had all the diseases of the world, and they had added an indication that of all these they only supported terminal illnesses, which we thought an odd way to express it. So much for the first section.

"The second indicated that they do not support institutions, organizations, associations, or individuals, nor do they provide collaborative support to projects of other funders.

"Thinking that we might slip in by calling ourselves a team, we took note of the other exceptions which fairly narrowly identified such factors as age, gender, geography, education, sexual preference, hobbies, physical attributes, IQ, and several other things.

"By the time we got to button three, we were a bit discouraged but we were glad we hadn't given up. The button was stiff from disuse, but we jiggled it free and heard a recorded message congratulating us on our extraordinary uniqueness. It ended 'We think the founder would have liked you.' With that, we were given a choice of filling out a multiple choice questionnaire or writing an instant essay. We all agreed that with three of us we'd have a better chance at multiple choice so we pushed button four."

At this point, Mr. Widen showed us a few of the pages that popped out:

1. We are an organization qualifying as:
   501 (C) (3)
   501 (C) (4)
   501 (C) (7)
   All or none of the above.
   We have our IRS letter to prove it.

2. We have been in business:
   500 years
   100–500 years
   50–100 years
   We are an emerging organization

3. Our role is:
   Direct service
   Advocacy
   Activism (If you check this box, don't bother to fill in the rest. We know your type.)

4. This project is for:
   Demonstration
   Demonstration and feasibility
   Demonstration, feasibility, modeling, and pilot
   None of the above, but we're innovative.

5. Please stipulate that on the basis of pre-research it is predictable that the project will do exactly what it says it will do, i.e., the project is actually finished, but it turned out so well that you think someone should have supported it in the first place. Please do not be afraid to be truthful. We like to back winners.

6. Would you describe the project as:
   Gamble?
   Flyer?
   Far out?

Please do not hesitate to check one of the above. It's the first one we look at and can save us all a lot of time.

"At that point we decided to do the essay," said Mr. Widen.

For ease in reporting, Mr. Widen and his team provided their essay, which follows:

Our organization is somewhere between emerging and well-established, but our grass roots already run deep and wide. We are innovative, but hold to traditional values. We are daring, but do not gamble. We do not believe in jargon or obfuscation. We are straightforward, solid, middle-of-the-road edgecutters with a record of feasibility pilots that model the best of demonstrations.

We do not seek project support that masks an underlying intent to build endowments or reserves, and we don't kid you with such blanket categories as contingency funds and demonstration projects. In perfect candor, what we seek is a plain ordinary Slush Fund.

We know that slush funds have gotten a bad name, but if you look at all the great organizations, Harvard, Metropolitan Museum of Art, Colonial Williamsburg, the Foreign Policy Association, and all the rest, what they all have in common are—liquid slush funds.

Any foundation worth its salt has its own slush fund—sometimes called the Officers' or President's Discretionary Fund.

Though the beauty of slush funds is that they trickle away, we are grant-smart enough to know that we should try to tell you what we *would* do with it which, of course, we don't know, which, of course, you know—all of which we both know.

A flexible, dynamic organization shouldn't try to foresee what's ahead, but must be ready to respond to the challenges and opportunities of the moment. Who would have planned or have been ready for the eruption of Mount St. Helens?

We can assure you that whatever unanticipated purposes we put your money toward will involve projects that can be replicated for meaningful implementation, employing the expertise of everyone in the community.

Right now, all of our ideas seem to need nourishment and, in keeping with the example and symbolism of the Green Revolution, good ideas, like crops, need the waters of spring, which, of course, come from mountain slush. Look upon our application as the Future Springs of Mount Everest Slush Fund.

You can be assured that the Board and staff of our organization are made up of average, middle-of-the-road plodders who are the type that de Tocqueville said made America what it is—and that have produced our country's pathfinders and explorers. Please do not turn us down because we are not already a rich, successful organization. Keep in mind that, before he took his flight, whoever heard of Lindbergh? And he didn't do it in some fancy multiengine jet. He chose a modest single-engine prop plane. That's our stage and style. You might even think of us as the Future Springs of Mount Everest Slush Fund to Nurture Later Lindberghs.

Lastly, we can assure you that no part of the grant will be used for overhead or fundraising costs. It will all be pure program expense composed of nothing but salaries and travel expenses and other basic costs of innovation.

If you need elaboration, let us know and we can shift some of the sentences around.

If you need a specific budget, we can make that up too.

Please send as much as you can as soon as you can.

We are a public charity with 501 (C) (3) status in reasonably good standing with the IRS.

Mr. Russell thanked Mr. Widen and his courageous team for their efforts to date. Mr. Gonzalez asked, "What happens next?" Mr. Widen indicated "If we pass the first stage, we get to meet a real person at the foundation." Louella Buckminster was so impressed that she wanted to know if we could all go. Mr. Widen downplayed the appointment and said that our team would probably just meet with a program officer. Mrs. Buckminster reacted, "That's still a lot better than an enlisted person or a civilian."

Mr. Colberg wanted to know, "How much are we asking for?" Mr. Widen explained that "We don't want to put in a specific figure, because you usually get only half of what you ask for and we're hoping for twice as much."

With the hour close to midnight, Mr. Russell suggested that we reluctantly skip the Program Committee report, the minutes, the Treasurer's report, evaluation of the Executive Director, and selection of the new Fundraising Chairperson. Recalling Jack Neal's note on our program report to National, Mr. Colberg commented, "The SOB was never so lucky." Mr. Widen was concerned that the organization would try to go as long as two months more without a new Fundraising Chairperson, but Bruce Knight assured him that, with all the money we would be getting from United Way, foundations, and bequests, we might not need a Fundraising Drive.

Despite the hour, several members were stunned that we would not get to the Treasurer's report. We would have been there until morning, but Mr. Russell reminded everyone that Mr. Gonzalez is bonded and through National we have directors' liability insurance for the Board. We were shocked to realize that we have any legal liability for what goes on here. We demanded that this topic be put high on the agenda of a future meeting.

I tried with all my might to get them to hear the minutes of the previous meeting, but all I could get was the Chairperson's assurance that very early in the next meeting we could have the minutes of the *two* previous meetings. I said that I thought it would be unconstitutional to do it that way. I thought Mr. Scala was about to agree with me when he said that he, too, thought it would be unconstitutional, "But," he added, "it will place us all in double jeopardy."

This unofficial meeting was adjourned at 12:01 A.M.

Angrily submitted,

Mrs. Jeffrey (Effie) Black
Secretary of the Board of Directors

Minutes of Our January Board Meeting

The meeting began at 8:08 P.M.

When asked to read the minutes of our last two meetings, I explained, just as I had in writing immediately following our informal gathering in November, that our failure to read and act upon the minutes of our September meeting disqualified both sessions as official. Mr. Russell cajoled, and Jack Neal pleaded, but I would not be budged. As far as I am concerned and as far as the records go, there was no September meeting and there was no November meeting, therefore there are no minutes to read.

Mr. Scala said that we ought to meet in secret more often and that we hadn't done anything worth recording anyway. Gladys Pepper brought him and everyone else to their senses when she asked whether this meant that our action on the bequest program wasn't being implemented. Jack Neal said tactfully that in the spirit of the Board's action, or at least consensus, he had already started visiting funeral homes. Mr. Colberg asked if it wasn't a little late for that, but Jack said he had gotten to it right after the meeting. Mr. Colberg asked if we were going to have an executive session.

I'm sure there was far more panic about the nonmeetings than showed, but, given the packed agenda, we moved on.

Our Treasurer had, as instructed, submitted his written statements in advance of the meeting. Paula Masonowitz handed them out at the door. Before Mr. Shapiro could pounce, Mr. Gonzalez alerted the group that, as part of his report, he also wanted to discuss with the Board a letter we had received from the IRS. With perfect timing and stage presence, he left that hanging for a good eleven seconds and then pretended to start back to the financials. All the while, Paula Masonowitz, among whose duties is the role of Assistant Treasurer, shook her head sorrowfully from side to side.

Their ruse worked. As if on cue, Mr. Horton wanted to know, "What letter?" . . . and off we galloped with only Mr. Colberg and Mr. Shapiro trying to rein us in with shouts of "Whoa there . . . hold up . . . just a minute now . . ." but they were dragged under the thundering stampede of IRS panic.

Mr. Gonzalez sat—staring at the letter—while the clamor rose to its crescendo and settled. At just the right moment, he raised the letter slightly and announced, in the tone he usually reserves for foreclosing mortgages, "They want proof that we're a public charity."

At first there was disbelief, and cries of "What does this mean?" . . . or worse, "Does this mean what I think it does?"

Then confusion turned to defensiveness and rebuttal, like, "Who could be more needy than us?"

And finally, and logically, it evolved to the inevitable

state of paranoia, with such normal reactions as, "They're out to get us."

Mr. Gonzalez seemed to have rehearsed even this part of the drama. With hands in the air, he called for quiet, and, just when we thought he was taking command of the situation, he announced, "I'm out . . . I quit." This was delivered in somewhat quaking but relatively level tones, quite unlike the outburst that followed: "Furthermore, you can count me out . . . forget it . . . who needs it . . . get yourself another boy . . . amscray . . . I can't take it another day . . . drop dead . . .," and miscellaneous other expressions, rising to such a pitch that the last several were inaudible—and probably just as well.

When calm was restored, Mr. Russell observed that in the face of the various expressions of reluctance and reservation, Mr. Gonzalez had won our sympathy. There was a round of applause—the first ever for our Treasurer.

Ms. Trister asked the obvious question: "What happens if we don't give the IRS a satisfactory answer?"

With funereal tones, Rev. Horsinger replied that we could lose our 501 (C) (3). Mrs. O'Reilly said that she had never heard it called that before. "I've heard it called bottom, fanny, butt, and even a naughty little word that begins with an 'a,' but even after raising six kids I've never heard it referred to by the numbers." Mr. Russell politely explained that the Reverend had not been speaking anatomically, and then everyone was confused. Know-it-all Mitchell said that losing one's 501 (C) (3) means we lose our tax exemption, which provided relief to most of the group, who obviously felt this was by far the lesser of the two evils.

"So what does that mean?" persisted Mrs. O'Reilly.

"It means," said Mr. Gonzalez, "we're out . . . kaput . . . done . . . finished . . . back to square one. . . ."

"OK, OK," intervened Mr. Russell, eager to avoid another of Harry's escalations.

Mrs. O'Reilly sorted it out this way: "As I understand it, it's taken all these years to work our way up to a 501 (C) or whatever and we could get shot all the way back to zero. What's wrong with starting back at one again, or couldn't we negotiate for a compromise and just go back to something in between, like 250 (L) (11)? Maybe our problem is that we got preoccupied with a false goal, like getting up to a 999 (X) (32), and it would be good for us to get shaken up with a little loss of status. Life belongs to those who respond to setbacks and who pick themselves up off the floor and start climbing again with grit and determination."

Mr. Gonzalez realized that even a primer on the tax code would be wasted on someone whose next goal in life was to go from 501 (C) (3) to become 501 (C) (4), so he settled for explaining that without what we have now, people couldn't deduct their contributions to our organization.

In an understandable but totally unsuccessful effort to return us to another fiscal subject, Mr. Shapiro responded, "If I take our financial report seriously, that would affect very few people!"

"But it would affect all of us around this table," said Mr. Colberg.

"How come?" queried Mr. Widen.

"If you had ever given a nickel to this organization, you wouldn't have to ask," snapped Mr. Colberg.

Mr. Widen, hurt, explained, "At the office, I just check off the box that says 'United Way,' and they deduct for me."

"But it still comes out of your pay."

"The hell it does."

"Of course it does, and you haven't even been taking

advantage of deducting it from your taxes, so the government has been keeping what it actually owed you."

Mr. Widen was crestfallen. "Isn't it awful to suddenly learn that the two groups you thought you could trust to do right by you, the United Way and the U.S. of A., have been in cahoots to take your money?"

Half of our group was unsettled to see a man so shattered, and the other half was shattered to see a man so unsettled.

We resolved the IRS issue by referring it to National.

Before moving on, Mr. Colberg wondered out loud how Gonzalez was going to top this performance in March to distract us from the financial report.

At that late point, Mr. Wenski arrived and explained that he had stopped to help a person with a dead battery, but because neither of them had jumper cables, they had to wait until someone else stopped who did.

Unruffled, our Chairperson reported for the Executive Committee. It had only met four times since our November gathering.

Mr. Russell said that they had covered a number of important items, some of which were so significant that he thought it best to ask the Board's blanket approval for what they had done and called upon me as Secretary of both the Board and Executive Committee to present a motion:

> On behalf of the Executive Committee, it is moved and seconded to approve the actions of the Executive Committee at its December and January meetings.

Mr. Horton inquired, "I don't suppose it would do any good to ask what specific actions we're voting on?"

"I'm afraid not," said Mr. Russell reluctantly. "You know the rules."

"I haven't been in a secret society since college," quipped Mrs. Pepper sarcastically. "Do you guys wear robes and call one another 'brother goblin'?"

Joining in what he thought was the merriment of her remark, Mr. Russell responded, "I guess that would make me the grand goblin," and he chuckled. Judging by Mrs. Pepper's stare of incredulous disbelief, it was clear that on at least this one occasion Mr. Russell had misjudged his Board's mood.

Quick to recover, he used the pained silence to suggest that hearing no further discussion, he would call for action on the motion. I could only catch two or three barely discernible "ayes" and Mr. Russell, sensing he was on shaky ground, wound down with a clever "Well, that should do it," and slipped into his Chairperson's report.

Later in the meeting, Mr. Colberg asked why the Executive Committee had not yet considered a budget for the year, and it was explained that this was among the items we had voted on in adopting the Executive Committee report. A motion to adjourn taking precedence, the howls of Mr. Colberg, Mr. Shapiro, et al. were overridden.

When we reassembled, Mr. Fales reported for his Annual Meeting Committee. The governor had been invited to speak but so far no answer had been received. Because the day was getting closer we needed to have a backup. Mrs. Greenlaw pointed out that this is exactly the same situation the organization has faced ten years in a row, and the governor hasn't shown up yet. Mr. Knight pointed out that this year the governor is a Republican. Mr. Scala wanted to know, "What the hell does that have to do with his showing up?" Mr. Knight said it was generally recognized that Republicans are more responsible. Mr. Russell reminded the group that we are nonpartisan.

When the group considered a substitute, just in case the Republican governor didn't show up, it was obvious that we should turn once again to our Founder, First Chairperson, and Chairperson Emeritus, who was persuaded to stand in for the governor. This would be the tenth year in a row that our community would have an opportunity to learn of the founding and earliest days of our association. When discussion turned to an award for the speaker, Mr. Peter Paul Henderson discreetly left the room. In his absence, it was agreed that we would have the plaque made up for the governor, but ask Hardy's Sport Shop to be ready to switch the simulated brass plate on the award at the last minute.

In the absence of Mrs. Mitchell (who was excused for being out of town, but in a different town than Mr. Zukert was excused for being in), Mr. Shapiro gave the report of the Personnel Committee, which had been asked to review the association's fringe benefit program, which presently includes social security, workman's compensation, and unemployment insurance. At our last review, Mr. Yarborough said, "That sounds pretty generous to me," and the matter would have rested there. That was before the state convention, where some of our delegates heard that a lot of chapters provide basic health coverage and a few of the bigger ones even have a retirement plan. One chapter was viewed as being way out of line because it provides death and dismemberment insurance.

"Disgusting!" said Mrs. O'Reilly, but we weren't sure which of the extremes she was referring to.

Mr. Horton thought that all this sounded like the typical soft-hearted socialist behavior of nonprofit organizations, in which people should be willing to make a real sacrifice. Mrs. Workenthrader asked if his employer provided a good benefits package, and he responded, "Yes, but that's business—and besides, in business, where the bottom line is the name of the game, our necks are on the block twenty-four hours a day, every day, so there have to be some incentives."

Rev. Horsinger was moved to unnatural annoyance and, apologizing that his children liked to eat and that they sometimes get hurt and bleed, said that his church had begun to actually pay him (if collections warrant) and let him have basic health coverage. That did it. Right then and there the Personnel Committee was instructed to do its review.

At this meeting, Mr. Shapiro cleverly picked up where the first discussion had left off. "Ladies and gentlemen, our committee has taken its guidelines from the situation represented by the Reverend Horsinger . . ."

But before he could continue, Mr. Horton blurted out, "My God, we're going to buy Jack a house."

After careful study, the Committee recommended that our chapter provide basic health coverage, with a $250 deductible per episode, and that this be available to all people who have been on the staff for at least five years. As an extra benefit, the coverage can be extended to families as long as the employee pays the family share. Further, the Committee proposed that we go to a 50-50 payment plan on Major Medical, $5,000 deductible per episode, for persons who have been on the staff ten years or more and that for long-term employees a retirement plan be provided with the association matching the employee's contributions one to five as long as the whole sum is returned to the organization if the person doesn't stay until age seventy.

"Why that last part?" asked Ms. Trister.

"That's so the person is sure to stay 'til seventy," responded Mr. Shapiro.

With an eye on Jack, Mr. Colberg pleaded, "You haven't said enough about dismemberment."

Mindful not to incur Rev. Horsinger's wrath, Mr. Knight

asked delicately if the Committee knew what this outlandish package might cost. Mr. Shapiro responded that the Committee knew that the Board wouldn't buy it all but had introduced it as an initial bargaining point and when the Board indicated what it might accept as a maximum, then prices would be secured and a fuller report would be presented to the Board. He said there was no rush because none of the staff was sick.

Further discussion revealed that the Board wanted the Committee to tone down some of the flashier coverage and bring in a recommendation with cost figures at a future meeting. Six amendments or substitutes to the motion for further study were defeated. Each would have required that, in case coverage is voted, we would do it through a specific friend or firm. Unfortunately, all six proposals were different. Mr. Shapiro suggested that the final plan be submitted for bids, but those who had offered the motions made clear that most agents don't do business with nonprofits that way.

Mr. Russell asked if there were any further business from the Personnel Committee, and Mr. Shapiro said that the only other item was a dress code for the office, but because the absent Chairperson, Mrs. Mitchell, was so enthusiastic about this item, he preferred that it be left until she could be present. Paula Masonowitz crossed a trousered leg and glowered.

With considerable fanfare and apologies for past postponements, our Chairperson called on Mrs. Archer to give the report of the Program Committee, but she was so surprised to actually have a chance to give the report that she was unprepared. She said that she might be able to get her thoughts together if he could come back to her.

It should be noted that her lack of preparedness struck a blow to her ambitions to head the organization in the near future. Some had even thought she was in a contest with Penelope Mitchell to replace Rodney Russell (though it should be noted that others saw it as a three-woman race, there being another female officer who should not be overlooked!).

While Mrs. Archer and Jack Neal began to huddle, Mr. Russell asked if there were any shorter items we could get out of the way. Ms. Trister reminded him that we still had not taken up the recommendation of her Bylaws Committee relating to whether the organization should use the term Chairman, Chairwoman, Chairperson, or Chair. But, with full support of the Board, Mr. Russell ruled that this could hardly be resolved with dispatch.

Mr. Scala mentioned that we had tabled an earlier discussion about whether or not to combine the Public Relations and Public Education Committees and that because this seemed like such an obvious move, he thought we could slip it in now. Out of both corners of his eyes, Mr. Russell saw the two rival Chairpersons beginning to rise with nostrils flaring, teeth bared, and eyes flashing, and said, "No, what I had in mind was something easier."

Any doubts about the mistake he had made to open the floor were sealed when Mrs. Lortz said that she would like to reopen the proposal for an auxiliary. He answered that we would wait for the Program Committee report with a break.

On reconvening, Mr. Russell asked Mrs. Archer if she was now ready, and with her return to confidence and positiveness she replied that it was a question of whether or not the Board was ready for a blockbuster of a report from the Program Committee. Clearly, Mrs. Archer had caught her breath. Jack Neal had scurried to dust off the flip chart, and the two were poised.

"To begin with," began Archer, "the organization needs a crisper, clearer, dynamic statement of mission.

The one we've got now is strictly mush and doesn't do anything to position us at the starting gate with a sense of inspiration and energy. With apologies to the Public Relations Committee,"—and from the look on Mrs. Greenlaw's face more than apologies were needed—"we've gone outside the organization to get the advice of the very best PR-advertising-marketing minds in the community and can bring you their suggestion, which carries the unanimous recommendation of the full Program Committee."

And with that, and with a kind of sing-song "Da-dah," she turned to Jack who, on cue, flipped to the first page. Unfortunately, it had been so long since the presentation had been prepared that someone else had used the presentation book, and it was turned to this later entry:

STAFF NOTES ON BOARD REORGANIZATION

We Need:

More thinkers
More clout
More money
More doers

FULL OVERHAUL—and soon
We need revolution, not evolution

Jack, having flipped the chart, wasn't in a position to see it, and thinking he had unveiled the crisper, clearer, dynamic statement of mission, stood facing the Board, beaming proudly. Gradually, he realized something was wrong, and at first he thought they didn't care for the revised statement of mission, but something told him it was worse than that. As eyes began to move from the display chart to him, he moved his eyes from them to the display chart, and he decided that if there was a merciful

Lord, death would be instantaneous. Unfortunately, God was otherwise occupied.

I'll say this for Jack—he doesn't give up easily. He turned to the Board and, with absolutely the sickest grin imaginable, stammered, "Just some scribbles from the staff party." He might have gotten away with it, but his hands were shaking so violently that when he tried to flip the chart back to the correct pages, he sent the display, stand and all, crashing to the floor.

Perhaps symbolically, while he was down Mr. Colberg suggested that this might be a good time for the Board's own consideration of revolution. Our Chairperson, ever fair, realizing that what Mr. Colberg had in mind was more like execution, suggested that we get on with the Program Committee report and take up other matters when cooler heads might prevail. "We don't want cool heads," shouted Mr. Shapiro, "We want *his* head."

By now Paula had gotten the stand righted and the charts flipped to the proper place, and Ms. Trister, who disliked confrontation anyway, picked the first quiet moment to observe, "I like it—I *really* like it," and all heads turned to figure out what she could possibly find to like. Embarrassed by the uncharacteristic attention, she just pointed to the proposed statement of mission which was now on prominent display.

Perhaps because it required some thought, it tended to distract the group, even from murder. Rev. Horsinger, who understood that absorption with positive things would be calming and healing, was quick to pick up on Beth Trister's enthusiasm. "I think it's an absolute honey," he explained, and with that, there was a cacaphony of "just great . . . a real winner . . . motivational as hell . . . brief but right on target," and so on.

Mrs. Archer didn't want to jar the group's enthusiasm by suggesting that they actually vote on such a major matter, so she interjected soothingly, "We're not asking you to vote on this tonight, but we want you to think about it and have it in mind as I present the rest of the report." And think about it we would. It was the first unifying theme in a long time and could be just what we needed for harmony and thrust. For easy reference and in preparation for the big vote to come, here is the recommendation for our new mission statement:

> This community needs the good that Our Organization can do, so we should give it to them good.

Mrs. Archer explained to us that "like all good advertising, it doesn't present perfect grammar but it does grab, and, in advertising, as everybody knows, grabber is more important than grammar."

Moving quickly, and with some return of confidence, Mrs. Archer said that her second point also picked up on the lessons of PR and marketing and involved:

SYNERGISM

She said, "We have to move out from and on to our mission in lock step . . . as a common phalanx . . . as one cohort . . . integrating all of our activities and energies to maximize our opportunities and obligations meaningfully." Warming to her theme and its rapt reception, she added, "To put it another way, we should not only all be singing from the same hymn book, but from the same page and stanza, and all our voices will rise in harmonious thunder that will rock this community like it's never been rocked!"

Even Mrs. Greenlaw joined in the applause, but not without an audible aside: "Guess who wants to be the choirmaster!"

The report continued: "To make all this happen will require discipline, including hard choices on goals, hammering out measurable objectives, setting realistic timetables and budgets, and then using each of these Board meetings as a moment of truth to measure progress, including the evaluation of the performance of each and every Board member."

"That should get Jack his smaller Board," observed Mr. Scala. And some small cracks in the Board's enthusiasm began to appear.

Realizing she was hitting pretty close to home, and was in danger of losing her advantage, the Program Chairperson rushed ahead: "When we've put our own house in order we'll be ready to move out to do the networking that is the secret of good community organization." Jack Neal peeked at the underpage and, raising it inch by inch to doublecheck and then quintuplecheck what it said, turned it over, but, as he had for the past twenty minutes, he kept his face to the chart and away from the Board. At this point, he was looking at the word

NETWORKING.

Mrs. Archer rushed on: "We need to build our bridges and influence with others who can help carry our load into every nook and cranny of this county. Our mistake is that we've been trying to go it alone and no matter how good we are, the job is just too large. We need to enlist the support of the service clubs, PTA, student groups, women's organizations, auxiliaries, political organizations, fraternal lodges, and a host of others so that as they go about their activities, they will also be going about ours."

Mr. Fales offered a note of caution, reminding the group that they weren't altogether without experience at outreach. He reminded some of the older Board members and informed the newer ones that they had once taken assignments to meet with other organizations to spread the word and the load, but what had happened was that "we got outmaneuvered and spent most of the next year fulfilling the resulting commitments to sell ten thousand raffle tickets for the Knights of Columbus, canvass the whole west side of town for the Cancer Society, handle six junior highs and nine elementary schools for National Firefighters Month, staff the fair booths for Amnesty International, and four of us are still learning sign language. So much for networking. The wider we spread the net, the more work we get."

Mrs. Archer almost violently seized the initiative. "That's it!" she shouted. "That's exactly it! We've got to outsmart them, outwit them, outmaneuver them so that they end up doing our work, not the opposite."

"But shouldn't networking be a two-way street?" inquired Mr. Horton.

"Do you want to end up buying more jackets for the Little League?"

"I see your point."

"An evangelist goes out with zeal, passion, and conviction and comes back with sales of souls, not soles to sell."

Perhaps it was a bit of overkill, but to solidify her own sale Mrs. Archer capped it all with, "Whoever heard of a Mormon evangelist coming home a Catholic?"

Mrs. O'Reilly started to object, but the opposition's point was too well made to risk even small protest.

Besides, Mrs. Archer was already into her point on networking.

"Once we've proven our conviction, tenacity, and influence, we'll be ready to go into the schools and churches." There were several gasps, and Rev. Horsinger looked half-defensive and half-fascinated. He didn't want anyone adding to his already difficult load, but, on the other hand, he was curious how so many people did.

"What two groups really influence the behavior of our citizens as much as the schools and churches? We can make the case that concern for our cause is a matter of the whole person and the whole person is what the schools and churches strive to develop. With enough pressure, we can take advantage of the natural guilt that good teachers and ministers carry around for all their charges who don't turn out perfect and, with their defenses down, convince them that adopting our cause might make the real difference. Why, we can even get the School Board to make our subject mandatory and get the Council of Churches to give at least a week and maybe even a month to our aspect of public service and personal growth."

Speaking from his own bias, Rev. Horsinger asked whether it wasn't better "to leave it to the schools to teach fundamentals and the churches fundamentalism?"

Undeterred, Mrs. Archer came back with, "It's a well-known fact that it's hard to get the attention of a hungry man."

The Reverend, beginning to feel outmaneuvered, shouted, "What the dickens does that have to do with what we're trying to do?"

But Archer closed with, "People can just as easily be starved for love or culture or growth, and that's where we sneak in."

Sensing Rev. Horsinger's momentary helplessness, our Program Chairperson sprang to her last point and, like a conductor rising toward the crescendo, snapped a pointed finger at Jack for the next chart. Having previously checked it out, he unfolded it with a flourish:

WELL-DIRECTED SERVICES PRODUCE
WELL-DESERVED INCOME

If there had been any doubt about the Program Committee winning the day, it evaporated on that page.

The central and winning point was quite simply this: "There are a lot of people in this community who need what we've got, and we ought to give it best to those who are in a position to reward us. And here we're speaking of hundreds, if not thousands, of businesses in this community who are tired of giving to causes which are just doing good and which don't have much proof of how much good they do and certainly don't do much good for the businesses making the contributions."

The usually skeptical Mr. Knight found himself responding spontaneously, "Here here, it's about time someone realized that business responds to a quid pro quo." On the other hand, Mrs. Buckminster wondered if it wasn't the business of organizations like ours to serve those who can't afford help and to convince businesses that they should help, too.

"The name of the game is both," said Archer, leaving most of us a bit unnerved, but she won us back by pointing out that "if we do a good turn for business and they contribute lots of money to us for it, then we can increase our services to them and to others."

"The genius of it is mind-boggling," responded Mr. Wenski.

Mr. Knight almost finished the report for the Committee. "Instead of behaving like all these other whining charities with their hands out, we can go to businesses and offer them something they need, and who will they choose to give priority to when contribution time comes around? I'll tell you who. Our organization."

For the second time that night, there was applause, but this time it was robust and prolonged.

Mr. Shapiro said that maybe we ought to combine the Program and Fundraising Committees, which would have happened on the spot if the respected Rev. Horsinger hadn't said that perhaps that was premature.

In any case, Archer's stock had shot sky-high, and the Board had momentarily forgotten Jack Neal's "Notes on Board Reorganization." There was a sense that at last we were on our way.

We had already covered so many momentous decisions that we didn't have any more time and energy to take up the executive session for evaluation of the Executive Secretary. For a while it looked as though a minority would filibuster until we did, but the crisis was averted when Mr. Russell promised that it would be a major part of our next meeting.

With that additional crisis passed, we adjourned at 11:37 P.M.

Respectfully submitted,

Mrs. Jeffrey (Effie) Black
Secretary of the Board of Directors

Notes of Our Annual Meeting (Our Big Fifteenth!)

In recognition of the special occasion, this year's Annual Meeting was held at Charlie's Bar and Grill rather than our usual location.

The dinner meeting was slow getting started because the reception itself was somewhat delayed. The problem was that we had agreed to charge $7.47, in keeping with our theme, "Getting a Fast Start on Our Next Fifteen Years," but the office had forgotten to bring change, and Charlie said it was bad practice to commingle his. Each person had to stand in line until we could give them the right change. Some were willing to round it out at $7.50, which speeded things a little.

Though the delay seemed to upset a lot of people, it probably helped space things out because the bar arrangement presented its own backup. People had to stand in line to buy a drink ticket, then they had to stand in line to get their drink, and then they had to get in another line to turn in their ticket. It is against the house rules for the bartender to handle cash or tickets. Charlie is very careful.

People kept pointing out that the bulletin board downstairs announced that our meeting was scheduled for lunch rather than dinner. Mr. Scala commented, "Charlie must have heard how long our meetings go and planned accordingly." Mrs. Lortz proposed that we accept the announcement on face value and go home. Fortunately, we weren't formally assembled yet so a motion wasn't in order.

It was when Jack Neal tried to get us to sit down that it became obvious that the microphone wasn't working. He stood there waving his hands and people just waved back and got in line again.

It got our attention when Jack's twisting of the microphone produced such a piercing squeal that Mr. Gonzalez said "it felt like having a lobotomy." Mr. Shapiro said he hadn't known that part of our Treasurer's past but it helped to understand our financial reports.

During the course of the meeting, Charlie came up twenty-nine times to adjust the microphone, and his percentages worked out to about one-third momentary success, one-third an even more penetrating screech, and one-third no sound at all, which turned out to be by far the preferred result.

In honor of the special anniversary, we had also secured the services of a professional master of ceremonies. He wasn't our first choice, and someone said he wasn't even on the initial list of 172 possibilities, but he was the one who agreed to do it, so we felt indebted. It turned out that the only thing appropriate about the choice was that he matched our screaming microphone.

"Doc" Haven is a disk jockey for WOCK, which he described as "strictly hard rock." He was introduced as

"WOCK's Doc Jock," the host of "Crock of Rock," and with that he bounded to the microphone with such energy and shouting that we were more startled by him than by what he set the microphone to doing. Mr. Peter Paul Henderson, our Founder, First Chairperson, and Chairperson Emeritus, was seated at the place of honor next to the podium and reacted to "Doc Jock" as though he had just taken his first not-quite-conclusive jolt in the electric chair. He leaned back to get the full measure of this host of "Crock of Rock," and either because of the angle or the incomprehensibility of what he saw and heard, he just kept going until he disappeared behind the podium. At first only Mrs. Henderson noticed that he was gone.

The brief interruption, which was prolonged a bit by Mr. Henderson's reluctance to leave his shelter, gave "Doc Jock" a chance to glance at the script, quite obviously for the first time. With Mr. Henderson shaking, but hanging on beside him, our emcee called for the invocation by the person "who will be identifed later." Unfortunately, either the committee or staff—at that point it didn't matter which—had forgotten to identify the invocator, but when that became obvious, our professional performer took it in stride: "With the authority vested in me as a former altar boy, I declare we've got God's zap." Rev. Horsinger was the only one to bow his head, but he seemed to be weeping or perhaps asking forgiveness.

Next on the script was a musical presentation by the seventh grade of PS #17, which had been performing at a lot of public events since winning last December's Christmas Sing. They were wonderfully spirited as they marched in and took their practiced places according to sound and size. They had drawn their first breath for the opening note, but it became increasingly difficult to hold during the prolonged pause that followed. Ms. Florence Brady, the accompanist and director, didn't see a piano anywhere. Neither did anyone else. When called, Charlie explained that was because there wasn't one upstairs and no one had bothered to ask him to move one in. For the sake of the kids, he said, he would arrange to turn off the TV in the bar, "which will get a lot of the regulars pretty steamed up," and Ms. Brady could use the upright that they had downstairs for their Saturday night "sing-alongs." It took awhile for Charlie to gain the cooperation of people using the other meeting rooms and to quiet the protests of the regulars, but finally, if you strained, you could hear Ms. Brady pounding on the keys that worked, and with one of the older children filling in beautifully as choirmaster, our entertainers did their medley of Christmas carols.

When they were finished, there was hearty applause. We could even hear the people down in the bar clapping and cheering, but Charlie told some of us later that was because the TV was back on.

The host of "Crock of Rock" said he had a few announcements. The principal one was that the restrooms were out of order *but* alternatives had been planned for. "The men can use the Exxon station, which is to the right going out the front door, and the women can use Shell across the street."

I didn't need to check whether his directions were accurate, but from what happened next I'm glad I didn't need to go. "Doc Jock" said that while everyone was digging into the fruit cups, he would introduce the head table. He studied the script and lost some of his professional polish when he turned it on its side and then upside down and finally called Jack to help him sort it out, but it turned out he wasn't very good at "stage left and stage right" and that some of the people had been switched around or hadn't shown up yet.

He began "on your left," and held up his left hand, and

"on your right," and held up his right hand. "Let me begin with the person who 'will be identified later' and who gave us the invocation," he said.

From there it was all downhill. For the record, Mr. Russell is not Mrs. Mitchell, the mayor was not present, Jack Neal is not head of the Personnel Committee (though that might have been wishful thinking), and the people on the left were actually on the right, and the ones announced as sitting closest to him were actually farthest away. The only person he got right was our Founder, who you may recall had attracted his attention earlier, and who was among those most eager not to be identified in any way by or with "Doc Jock."

Our emcee was on a little safer ground when he said he wanted to acknowledge several special people seated out in the audience, but the result wasn't much better. It turned out not to matter that he so grossly mispronounced their names, because after calling twenty-three names and waiting for each person to stand and be recognized, none of them were present, though one did come later.

It was about that time that we were startled to hear what sounded like the Fourth of July parade coming right through the room. Unfortunately, it was not to be that brief. The room next door had been rented out for a drum and bugle competition, and we were hearing just the first of thirty-three groups. We ate our fruit cups while someone sent for Charlie, but when he came up he appeared to be straining to hear and, shouting over the din, announced, "I'm not sure I know what you mean, but I'll ask them to keep it a little quieter anyway."

That was the group to the right of us. It turned out that on the left, just cranking up, was the monthly meeting of the hard-of-hearing Toastmasters Club.

The mayor wasn't able to bring us personal greetings

but had arranged to send a substitute, who eased our disappointment by assuring us that he was a blood relative on the mayor's wife's side and had been the mayor's driver since the day His Honor took office. With those credentials, we were complimented to hear so much of the family's history in this country and in Italy, Ireland, and Lithuania. "Doc Jock" had thought to add a lighter note when he smilingly announced to the group, "And that only includes those whose mothers and fathers were married," but the mayor's driver took it seriously and explained that "it wouldn't be right to mention the bastards because so many of them are still living."

Fortunately, he got to the Proclamation, which provided a reminder that most of those who are called upon to read proclamations have not only not read them ahead of time, but can't pronounce many of the words. Proclamations are either too scholarly for those who read them or those who read them are too unschooled to handle them. There really ought to be a balance. Perhaps we should ask National to take this on as a service to the country.

By that point, we were aware of three things. One, it was going to be a very long evening; two, we were very hungry; and three, it was not to change film that the photographer had kept going down to the bar. At first we thought he was trying to take pictures at odd angles but it became increasingly obvious that it was he who was at odd angles. As the mayor's relative/driver/representative was leaving, some of us thought the photographer was trying to catch a series of running pictures, but in fact he had simply started to lean to the left and the only way he could remain even partially upright was to move faster and faster in that direction. Unfortunately, as I think they say in sports, when he went down, he took someone out with him, and, even more unfortunately, it was the waitress carrying the tray with our salads topped with Charlie's famous thick Russian dressing. As unfortunate as all that was, it was compounded when fifty-two salads with Charlie's famous thick Russian dressing landed on the United Way exec who had come to look us over. She (at least I think it was a she, it was hard to be sure at that point) seemed to take it with remarkably good spirits, though some said her laugh sounded a little hysterical.

Mr. Zukert predicted that "she might not hold it totally against us. At least she got to go home early."

Charlie was more concerned about his waitress than about us, and said, "Besides, he's your photographer, so don't blame me. Also besides, those were all the salads we've got, so you'll just have to wait for the main course."

Food seemed a dim prospect when the waitress announced that she "wasn't going to work with that nutty group a minute longer," and Charlie said he'd go to the bar to see if anyone was in condition to help out.

The only one not starving at this point was the new baby of our one-day-a-week bookkeeper/dictaphone-transcriber/telephone-operator and general handyperson, who had gotten so upset by the clamor that the only way to calm him was to breast-feed him a little ahead of schedule. Unfortunately, in the quiet that followed Charlie's announcement, people began to notice what was otherwise hardly noticeable, and the thing that became most noticeable was that we are not a very modern group. What was perhaps most noticeable of all was that once people noticed, they did everything possible not to seem to notice, and all the not noticing and the efforts to avoid anyone else noticing added up to rather noticeably bizarre head movements. It was like fifty-two people watching fifty-two different doubles matches.

Fearing that "Doc Jock" would compound the shock with one of his observations, and/or fearing that Peter

Paul Henderson would topple behind the podium again, our Chairperson interceded and called for a break, thoughtfully reminding everyone about the Exxon and Shell stations.

No sooner had we reassembled with what seemed like the comforting prospect of food, than a collective shriek began to build. It started with one or two people at one table and within seconds had spread to every table in the room. Some of us didn't comprehend but those who did were aghast. Mrs. O'Reilly made it clear for all of us. With a sharper and higher pitch than even the microphone had yet reached, she announced that "what we are all looking at is pot roast," which frankly sounded and looked pretty good to me, but she coupled it with "and may the Lord forgive us, it's Good Friday." The moral issue we faced was as profound as a group could possibly grapple with together. Some said things like "God would certainly understand," and others countered with things like "We'll all be damned."

For all his insensitivity, Charlie demonstrated why he could run both the bar *and* grill. Though we'd have to pay for it and he didn't have any on hand, he'd be willing to organize a group from the bar to get as many orders of fish and chips as we needed. It was an ideal solution, but we lost the better part of an hour while people made up their minds whether they would not eat pot roast as a gesture of symbolic support or would eat pot roast because they were starved, and while we worked out the reimbursement that people would get because they weren't eating pot roast ("And shouldn't we get money back for the salads too?"), and while we figured out how many wanted their fish and chips with ketchup and how many with vinegar. The dilemma involved in the symbolic protest was decided for most of us when the group agreed, by a vote of thirty to twenty-two, that the only people who could get reimbursed were those whose faith actually prohibited them from eating the pot roast. Symbolism is never very substantive anyway.

The next question was whether those who had the pot roast and *were* going to eat it should go ahead or wait until the others got their fish and chips. That vote was fairly decisive, so most of us ate while the others watched. They got back at us because the pot roast was terrible and we had to sit and watch them eat what looked like delicious fish and chips. Rev. Horsinger observed, "God works in mysterious ways." We were all thoughtful.

To make up for lost time, we moved right ahead with the Nominating Committee report. Mr. Russell explained that the Board elects its own officers, so the only role for the membership is to fill vacancies on the Board. On behalf of the Nominating Committee, Mr. Yarborough called for the reelection of all the current Board members and submitted three names for the vacancies. Two of those nominated were present but hadn't known they were being proposed, and both declined. Mrs. Plimpton had the good grace to say that her schedule just couldn't permit it, but Mr. Fleishman was overheard to say, "It's bad enough just coming to Annual Meetings." Speaking for the third person an associate said, "There wasn't a chance in the world of his considering it." So we were back to the renominations.

Gloria Morrison asked if nominations could be made from the floor, but we all knew who she had in mind, and Mr. Yarborough alertly pointed out that nominations have to be made in advance. Mrs. Morrison noted, "Those two people didn't know in advance," but Mr. Yarborough said, "That's OK. The Nominating Committee knew."

When Mr. Yarborough asked for a vote on the reelections, Mrs. Morrison asked, "Do we have a policy on rotation and, if not, shouldn't we have?" Mr. Peter Paul

Henderson said he would be covering that in his address, which he didn't, but he carried the moment. Our loyal little band was reelected.

The master of ceremonies gave a big buildup to the next person: "It's now time to introduce the *real* leader of this organization, who will give us our marching orders not just for the next year but for the next fifteen years. And now I call on that person to come forward."

Unfortunately, Mr. Henderson, Mr. Russell, and Jack Neal all started for the podium at the very same instant, and when that became obvious to each of them, they froze in embarrassment and horror and might have been in that position even now if "Doc Jock" hadn't come to the rescue with, "That's what I call teamwork. No wonder this organization has such depth of leadership. I think they all deserve a round of applause."

Out of a relief that we had all survived a shared crisis, the applause was thunderous. It also saved our having to hear the usual reports of our Chairperson and Executive Secretary.

As planned, there was a break in the heavy business. With a deserved flourish and fanfare, the host of "Crock of Rock" introduced the winner of the AmVets Region 14 oratorical contest, "who at fifteen is clearly destined for national leadership." In ringing tones, the boy delivered his winning oration, "Without Wars, There Are No Heroes." It was hard to get back to business.

Mr. Russell took the chair at this point to call for committee reports. He reminded the eleven committee heads that each had been asked to limit presentations to no more than five minutes. Mrs. Archer came closest to the limit with eleven-and-a-half minutes, and Mrs. Mitchell broke her own record of last year.

Charlie began coming up about every fifteen minutes to see if we were done yet, which made it a bit nerve-racking, but that was offset by having outlasted the drum and bugle competition.

Fortunately, the awards went fairly quickly. It became obvious that Jack Neal was not giving them to "Doc Jock" in the same order as "Doc Jock" was announcing them, and the swapping and confusion got a little complicated, along with trying to get people to agree to take the awards to most of the winners who weren't there anyway. Mr. Russell intervened again and asked everybody to turn in the awards distributed so far and assured everybody that they would be mailed to the proper people within a few days.

Mr. Colberg asked if we ever had executive sessions at Annual Meetings. Our master of ceremonies looked confused, so Mr. Russell said, "Don't worry about it, it's a little 'in' joke," but Jack Neal didn't laugh.

This brought us to the high point of the meeting, the address of our Founder, First Chairperson, and Chairperson Emeritus, who gave even the Region 14 winner a lesson in gilded oratory, along with a very detailed review of the history of "Our Organization." For those who have minutes from any of the last nine Annual Meetings, you'll find a copy of pretty much the same address attached to them. For others, a copy of the annual address is available from the office.

As soon as Mr. Henderson finished, he was somewhat startled by the standing ovation, but it was clear that most people were using this as an excuse to move toward the door. "Doc Jock" stopped them in their tracks by reminding them that the state president was present to participate in this fifteenth anniversary and to make a surprise award. Geoffrey Mawby announced that in recognition of our Founder's extraordinary record of service, the state association was adding a seventy-eighth award to its list of special presentations made at each state convention.

The new award will be named for Peter Paul Henderson and will be given each year to the oldest person with the longest continuous record of service who was finally going off a chapter or state board. Some of us thought this was a mixed message, but the important thing was that Mr. Henderson thought it was wonderful.

It set us in the mood for the most serious item of business, the resolutions. None had been submitted in advance, but three came from the floor, two of which were serious and none of which were taken seriously. The first was from a Board member, of all people. Mr. Zukert submitted a proposal "that we not have Annual Meetings anymore." Charlie, though out of order as a nonmember, added an amendment "that at least you not have an Annual Meeting at Charlie's anymore." Mrs. Morrison suggested that we limit the terms of Board members and that the Nominating Committee be instructed to seek "new blood" to counter the "dry rot." Mr. Henderson winced, but we were not sure whether it was in response to the language or the substance.

The voice vote on Mrs. Morrison's resolution was challenged by Mrs. Morrison. The show of hands was not any more conclusive. The standing vote was questioned on the grounds that several people were simply stretching or leaving and we didn't have paper and pencils for a written vote. Beth Trister, though a newcomer, proved that she had learned her Robert's Rules by calling for a motion to adjourn. Mrs. Morrison said that was illegal. Charlie said we were all going to jail anyway if we didn't get out. We looked around and realized that other than Mrs. Morrison, the only ones left were Board members, so we agreed we'd reopen her resolution at the next Board meeting. Mrs. Morrison saved us the trouble by concluding, "Don't bother."

Charlie usurped the authority of both the emcee and

our Chairperson by announcing, "You are adjourned. And be sure to take your photographer with you." The photographer was the only one still smiling, but he probably didn't even know it.

We dragged him and ourselves out at 1:17 A.M.

Respectfully submitted,

Mrs. Jeffrey (Effie) Black
Secretary of the Board of Directors

Minutes of Our March Board Meeting

The meeting opened at 8:21 P.M. after we waited an extra fifteen or twenty minutes for Mr. Peter Paul Henderson to arrive. Fearing the worst, Mr. Russell called Mrs. Henderson, who said that our Founding Chairperson had sprained his neck at the Annual Meeting and would have to miss his first meeting in fifteen years. She said that he thought about trying to make it, but both of them agreed it could jeopardize his suit against the association.

Mr. Russell reported to everyone that Mr. Henderson was much better, which was good news by itself but also because it reduced the chances that the suit would involve death benefits.

We all agreed that it seemed strange not to have our Founder, First Chairperson, and Chairperson Emeritus at the table, and mostly nice things were said about him. After everyone had said all the nice things they could think of and there was one of those long pauses you learn to recognize as preamble to what's really on peoples' minds, Mr. Scala said that maybe this was our one and only time to talk about how to get rid of him. For the next fifteen minutes, everyone's sentence began with something like "I know how much he has meant to the organization, *but* . . . ," or "No one is more devoted to Mr. Henderson than I am, *but* . . . ," or "I owe everything I've learned about this community to him, *but* . . . ." After a while, the prefaces changed to statements like "It looks like the old goat is going to live forever so we'd better . . . ," or "We may never have the chance again to get out from under that crazy dictator so we'd better. . . ." Finally, people just let it all hang out, including every single one of the people who had opened the discussion with such praise. Left to cook long enough, toasts turn to roasts.

Mrs. Archer admitted that she dreaded having to sit beside him because "he seems to have only three ways of reacting to things. Depending on how strongly he feels, he scowls, shakes his head, or spits up."

Mr. Widen recalled "the time someone suggested we be willing to change our name to conform with National's resolution and Mr. Henderson actually convulsed and Mr. McDonald had to give him CPR. That was really rough. Besides, McDonald has never been back."

Mr. Fales complained that Mr. Henderson always treated the organization like he owned it and made everybody else feel like an intruder. "He counters every suggestion he doesn't care for with something like, 'The founders would be aghast,' or 'We who were there at the beginning never would have countenanced this, or worse, 'We don't do it that way.' "

Mr. Yarborough agreed that it was difficult "having him always sitting there staring and disapproving. Hell, it's like having your grandfather propped up in your bedroom." Mrs. Workenthrader interjected, "If that had been your situation, you would never have had eleven kids."

For the rest of our discussion, it wasn't a question whether he should go, but who would tell him. There has never been a more telling test whether an organization is made up of volunteers. When Mr. Russell suggested we draw straws, the tenor of the discussion switched back to sweetness and light, as twenty out of twenty-one withdrew themselves from consideration with such disqualifications as, "He's been so good to me that I shouldn't be . . . ," or "As his principal backer on the Board, I shouldn't be . . . ," or "As one who roomed with him at the state convention, I shouldn't be. . . ."

Mr. Widen said we could impose an attendance requirement and tell him he had fallen under the limit, but even our Founder's worst critics agreed that eighty-four out of eighty-five is not bad.

We thought we had hit on the solution when Mr. Knight suggested we get National to tell us that it is policy that everyone has to rotate off after six or eight years, but Mrs. Mitchell pointed out that half the National Board has been on thirty or more years, so that wouldn't work.

The next best thing was to vote to hire an objective outside independent management consultant who would give us strict advice that no person could serve more than ten consecutive years. Like binding arbitration, we would agree that we would have to accept the advice. Ms. Trister asked naively how we could be so sure that an objective outside independent consultant would reach that conclusion, and Mr. Horton responded disdainfully, "That's easy . . . you just hire them with that understanding."

Ms. Trister didn't want to challenge further Mr. Horton's worldliness, but without backing all the way down she asked, "What if our Founder, First Chairperson, and Chairperson Emeritus challenges the decision?" Mr. Russell responded with his own worldly observation, "We'll cross that bridge when we come to it."

The Board moved on with a new sense of both worldliness and independence.

I was not even given the courtesy of beginning the minutes before Mrs. Lortz cut in to complain that they did not reflect her eleven corrections and her point of personal privilege relating to the prior minutes. "The current minutes," she shrieked, "only reflect three of the gross errors I pointed out in the record of our earlier meeting and certainly do not adequately represent the matter of personal privilege."

Keeping my cool, I responded with business-like iciness that I had carefully studied all of her eleven suggestions and had found six inconsequential, two bordering on nit picking and, in the case of the misspelled word, Webster says either is correct. On that basis I had not felt it appropriate to include in the minutes her motion citing the secretary "as both sloppy and a miserable speller."

Defeated on those counts, Mrs. Lortz hammered away at the issue of personal privilege. Pounding the table she said, "I don't think that the Secretary should be allowed to express a personal grudge in the minutes and I move that all such references be deleted from the minutes of the past two meetings." Mr. Russell asked if she would be more explicit and Mrs. Lortz responded that for the minutes of two meetings ago she had objected to the description, "Mrs. Lortz as usual, provided a biting reaction to almost every issue." She said that the Chairperson's instructions to change it were hardly reflected in the new description, "Fortunately, at this meeting Mrs. Lortz was preoccupied with a ferocious attack on her own fingernails and knuckles."

The fact that the Chairperson agreed with the accuracy of my statement did little to appease Mrs. Lortz who compounded her own parliamentary maneuvering by offering both a debatable and non-debatable item in the same motion "As a matter of personal privilege (nondebatable) I demand that the minutes be changed and further I call for the Secretary's public apology, which if not forthcoming should lead to her dismissal (debatable—but laughable)."

Amendments, substitute motions and motions to divide began to pile up. Mr. Russell realized that all of us were in parliamentary quicksand. Recalling earlier debacles fed by ignorance of the Rules, he called for a cessation of hostilities while we reviewed some basics of orderly debate. Most pressing was understanding what is debatable and what is not.

Mrs. O'Reilly who had seen the movie "Twelve Angry Men" about a jury and therefore came as close to an expert as anyone in the room, gave this outline of motions that are not debatable, along with her own practical examples.

"To protest a breach of rules or conduct"	As in, "She's pulling my hair!?!"
"To call for an intermission"	As in, "With all this coffee doesn't anyone else need to . . . ?"
"To complain about conditions"	As in, "This heat is so bad, my underwear is sticking!"
"To avoid considering an improper matter"	As in, "I agree we should all be concerned about fluoridation, but, after all, this is an Association of Grandmothers for Planned Parenthood!"

"To confirm a decision by calling for a standing vote"	As in, "I know it sounded unanimous, but with this crazy person in the chair it's the only way we're ever going to get to stretch!"
"To call for a point of in-formation"	As in, "Are you out of your cotton-pick'n mind?"

Armed with this and other new intelligence, twenty-one members of the Board offered their own nondebatable motions, each of which took precedence over the others. Our Chairperson rose to the moment with shifty-eyed sagacity and chose to hear only the call for an intermission, which he reminded the group was not only not debatable but did not even require a vote.

When he returned to the table fifteen minutes later, having been the only one to leave the table or the discussion, Mr. Russell announced that we would move on to the only topic which people were even more determined to tackle, the Treasurer's report. He even leavened the transition with a bit of humor, though Mr. Gonzalez didn't see it that way. "Now we can stop throttling one another and all throttle the Treasurer." There was nervous laughter.

Mr. Gonzalez held a different report in each hand, as though weighing their contents and a decision how to proceed. Mr. Colberg, suspecting another dodge, announced, "I'm not going to play enee-meenee-minie-mo with you, Gonzalez, let's get the bad news over with."

Unruffled, Mr. Gonzalez said, "I agree entirely that our time should be spent on the current figures, but I was just wondering if it wouldn't make sense to get the investment policies out of the way first. At the last meeting, with the prospect of a surge of income coming at us from several sources, you asked me to give thought to what we would do with all that income. It's really fairly straightforward, so perhaps I should get your nod on that and then go on to more immediate issues."

His timing and judgment were perfect once again. Before he had gotten halfway through the sentence, that handout was already on its way around the table, and knowing that most people were far more interested in investments than deficits, he had double momentum.

Though it may have been an empty gesture, he offered to quiet the protest by also distributing the handout of the financial statements but was saved from it by a chorus of: "No, let's get investments behind us first."

The recommendations *were* pretty straightforward:

Available Cash and Other Liquid Assets	Recommended Disposition
First $5,000 of petty cash	Non-interest-bearing checking account
Cash Flow Monthly Needs—$5,000–$25,000	Non-interest-bearing checking account
$25,000–$50,000	Savings account—current yield, 1.7 percent
$50,000–$100,000	Money market account—current yield, 2.1 percent
$100,000–$500,000	Certificates of deposit—current yield, 2.6 percent
Over $.5 million	U.S. Treasury Bills ("May be too risky")

After we had a chance to look this over, but before anyone could comment, Mr. Gonzalez reminded us that, as both our banker and our Treasurer, he has a responsibility to recommend a prudent investment strategy and, after pausing, he intoned that we, as trustees, must keep in mind our fiduciary responsibilities. He ended by reminding us of our earlier discussions and concerns about legal liability. "And, of course, the greatest strength and safety is to deal with a bank insured by the Federal Deposit Insurance Corporation—FDIC."

Ever alert and optimistic, Beth Trister jumped in with, "What about sums that exceed the $100,000 FDIC limit?"

Most of us would have guessed that he could have gotten by with, "We'll cross that bridge when we come to it," but he won our confidence when he responded in candor, "I can arrange to spread the extra around."

Mr. Shapiro had done some quick figuring and judged that "if we had a million dollars, we'd probably be earning about 4-1/4 percent when we could be getting closer to twelve percent."

"Yes," shot back our Treasurer, "But you'd be sacrificing the strength and safety of a bank."

"I don't think you stated that quite accurately," snapped Shapiro. "It would be *contributing* to the strength and safety of a bank."

"Have it your way," sighed Gonzalez, "but I wouldn't want the responsibility of being Treasurer in an organization that blew a million dollars."

"It hasn't bothered you until now," observed Mr. Colberg.

"What other options do we have?" asked Mrs. Archer.

Mr. Gonzalez responded: "I suppose we could put it in a trunk and bury it," which brought a few smiles, but the matter was too serious for laughs.

Mr. Zukert said, "We could go for 'total return.' "

"I don't know what that is, but I like the sound of it," said Mrs. O'Reilly.

Mr. Zukert explained: "The concept allows you to invest in a combination of accounts, including common stocks, and to try to produce a predictable annual yield for current operations. In this way you get the benefit of some of the income and also have a hedge against inflation."

It was clear that Mrs. O'Reilly didn't grasp the concept, but the idea of "total return" held enormous appeal, so she asked the Treasurer, "Who could be against our getting everything returned?"

"If you want it on your conscience that you've put public funds entrusted to you into *common* stocks, that's your business," warned Gonzalez, and it was obvious to everyone that he had immediately corralled the group toward his original proposal. Mrs. Mitchell spoke for the group: "I think we'd all be more comfortable if we followed the most careful, cautious, and conservative plan."

"We could take turns carrying it around in our shoes," cracked Mr. Scala.

"Knowing us, they would be open-toed," quipped Mrs. Pepper.

The matter was resolved for the interim by agreeing that we would use the early part of our windfall to deal with the deficit, and then several chimed in, "We'll cross that bridge when we come to it."

Mrs. Mitchell asked if we shouldn't plan to pay off some of our past dues to National, and this momentarily struck a guilty chord which was quickly assuaged with an understanding that "when our reserves get above one quarter of a million, we'll try to negotiate our debt for ten cents on the dollar."

The always practical Rev. Horsinger asked if any of the money had begun flowing in yet, and Jack Neal responded, "We're beginning to see some signs." Mr. Colberg asked what that meant and Jack responded, "Some dribs and drabs."

Mr. Shapiro persisted, "Could you be a bit more specific?"

Jack said, "This week we got a check for $25, a check for $10, a check for $5, and then a lot of little ones."

Mr. Colberg sighed, and Mr. Shapiro cried, and Mr. Russell realized there was no sense getting any deeper into the current state of financial affairs. Not wanting to appear irresponsible, he concluded, "If things haven't turned around by June, we'll have to take a hard look."

With that ninety-day reprieve, even Mr. Gonzalez and Jack nodded agreement, and Mr. Russell picked up the pace.

Mr. Knight reported on our visit to a corporate chief executive officer (CEO). Throughout Mr. Knight's presentation, he was mindful of Mr. Horton's hurt feelings when we had first talked about "getting some *real* corporate clout on our Board." As delicately as possible, Mr. Knight reminded us that we had decided we should strike for some high-level corporate CEO for the Board with the expectation that he (why must they always use *he*?) would bring swarms of his peers on too. Mr. Knight continued, "In addition to getting his own participation we need to get that first corporation on board as a substantial contributor, and we need to crack their payroll deduction, where the big bucks are. Also, once we get those big boys with us they do all kinds of other things like help with printing, gifts of equipment, loaned executives, use of boardrooms ("I'd like that," interjected Mrs. Mitchell) and all kinds of other things."

Mr. Knight said that the only way they had been able to make the appointment was to assure the CEO that we were not approaching him to be on our Board, or to provide corporate support, or to be part of their in-plant solicitation, or for any other tangible assistance but that we just needed ten minutes of his time to get his advice.

With that, Mr. Knight seemed to stammer a bit, causing Mr. Yarborough to ask "Well, what were you able to get?"

"We got twenty minutes."

"That's terrific, but what did he give us?"

"We got lots of good advice."

"Is that all?"

"By no means. We got our foot in the door and that's about all we could expect on a first visit. Besides, he said that if their situation changes he will surely let us know."

"What do you mean 'changes'?"

'Well, right now all their corporate executives are tied up with community responsibilities with several commitments on line. Their in-plant solicitation is reserved for United Way but he's pleased that we'll be part of that system and can participate with them in that way. He likes the idea of our doing services for companies and thinks that's a good way to win support, but he suggested we start with some of the smaller companies first."

It was obvious that Mr. Knight was coming to another awkward juncture. Putting a good face on it, he added that the CEO said that "if it would help to have their deputy assistant Zone 17 sales manager on the board, he'd broach it. . . ."

No sooner was that out than the sullen Mr. Horton protested, "That lowly cricket isn't as high over there as I am in my company, and the CEO knows that."

Mr. Knight fumbled, "I'm afraid it was obvious that the CEO doesn't know you."

"That's absurd," protested Horton. "We were at the same ball once!"

The awkward silence was broken by Mrs. O'Reilly, who observed, "I guess you should have asked him to dance."

The deputy assistant Zone 17 sales manager was referred to the Nominating Committee.

Mrs. Workenthrader reported for her team, which had

been assigned to visit the Voluntary Action Center (VAC). This part of the meeting also *started* well.

"I know most of you are familiar with what a VAC does but to bring us all up to speed, the Center helps to recruit, train, and place volunteers in meaningful community assignments. It's kind of a broker between volunteers who are willing to give their time and the organizations that can use that time well."

That part sounded good to us, but the compact is a little more exacting than some of us figured.

"We met with the Director of the Center, who explained that they have to be satisfied that an organization *really* is ready to utilize the volunteers effectively and to give them a sense of being part of the team in an important endeavor."

Mr. Fales picked up on the reporting: "It seems we can't just call over there for clerical help when we need it. They were quite definite that they are not the 'Kelly Girls for Free' service."

Already our group was losing interest.

Ms. Trister was curious: "Well, what *would* they do for us?"

Mrs. Workenthrader outlined: "If they are satisfied that we need volunteers for the good of our cause and have carefully thought through their orientation, training, and supervision, VAC wants to work with us. They'll also need assurances that their volunteers will be given opportunities for advancement and for fullest use of their talents and experience in helping us build every aspect of the organization."

"I thought they were just volunteers," responded Mrs. O'Reilly.

"Sounds kind of pushy," added Mrs. Archer.

Mrs. Mitchell went on: "They wanted me there as head of the Personnel Committee, though for the life of me I couldn't figure out why. It turns out they expect a work contract, job descriptions, evaluation procedures, and a lot of things we haven't gotten around to even for the staff."

"Sounds like they're not willing to do scut work anymore," said Mr. Yarborough.

"That doesn't seem to be it," replied Mrs. Workenthrader. "The Director assures us that their people are willing to dig in at every level of the organization, as long as they know it's important and feel that they are respected as individuals and as part of the team."

"When you come to think of it, that doesn't seem unreasonable," observed Rev. Horsinger.

"But they'd be getting more than the Board gets," replied Mrs. Lortz.

"Or the staff," added Jack.

After further discussion, a motion was passed "to thank the VAC for its time and interest but to indicate that at this stage our organization is not ready for volunteers."

While Mrs. Mitchell had the floor, she asked to continue with the Personnel Committee's report, which also dealt with the office move.

Mrs. Mitchell said that with the end of our one-year lease, it was time again to look for new quarters. Mr. Shapiro reacted, "Not again! Why in the world do we go through this about every year?"

Mrs. Mitchell explained that "to get the best deal, we generally look for situations where someone has temporary space which they are willing to let us have at below market cost. In the present case, the Safeway store is ready to open its bakery department so we have to move again."

Mr. Shapiro asked, "Wouldn't it make more sense to spend a little more and not use up so much of our energy with these constant moves?" But Mr. Zukert said he couldn't believe where this suggestion was coming from.

Mr. Shapiro defended himself by talking about "false economies," though he acknowledged that "any show of economy would be welcome around here."

Mrs. Mitchell admitted that her committee was badly split on the issue of whether to spend more and even whether to spend enough to get a location that would give us visibility and prestige.

"My God, I can hear Main Street coming next!" exclaimed Mr. Colberg.

"Well, as strange as that may seem, we actually have had that listed as one of our options," chimed in Mr. Fales, a member of the committee. "Some of us feel that maybe part of our problem is that we keep acting poor when maybe we should take off our hair shirt and strut a bit."

"You have to get your legs under you before you can strut," observed Mr. Shapiro profoundly.

For thirty minutes the Board went back and forth on the relative public relations of having the look of success as contrasted with the trappings of charity. Mrs. Greenlaw, commenting for the Public Relations Committee, provided a Solomon-like solution: "It should be right smack in the center of things for maximum visibility but semi-seedy so that people will want to help us."

"How about a tent on the Common?" offered Mr. Scala, and we all enjoyed the lighter moment, except maybe the staff. Mrs. Archer said she heard United Way may have some extra space, but several Board members recoiled. They said that it was one thing to belong to United Way to get money from them and quite another to give them the opportunity for complete control. "We need our independence more than we need their money," championed Mr. Widen, but others seemed to be pondering where that logic led.

Some others inquired whether there might not be some benefit in going in with several other organizations to pool the rent so there could be better space and shared services. Jack Neal countered, "The disadvantage with that is that a lot of small organizations get to take advantage of all our know-how."

The pondering became more pondered.

Before we had resolved such matters as location and relative poverty, we found ourselves drawn into more everyday issues, such as furniture, equipment, and decorations.

"I don't care what we do as long as we get rid of these crippling chairs," pleaded Mrs. O'Reilly. "And this table that keeps running my stockings," added Mrs. Buckminster.

"And while we're on priorities, let's never again use that sick green color on the walls. It's the one thing that seems constant about our offices," said Mr. Yarborough.

"One of the Board members sold it to us by the drum," said Jack, "and we weren't sure whether we should give priority to conflict of interest or long-term commitment to sick green."

"Maybe that's why Mr. Henderson gets sick to his stomach," observed Ms. Trister.

"No, he was doing that before someone unloaded that paint on us," said Mrs. Lortz.

"Maybe it would help him and all of us if we had some windows next time," pleaded Rev. Horsinger.

"Next thing you know, you'll want stained glass and we won't be able to see out anyway," said Mr. Scala.

Windows led to curtains (Mrs. Archer thinks she has some old ones in the attic) and to other nice touches that would make it seem more homey. Concerns about cost were dispelled when the group volunteered to canvas garage sales for furniture—and maybe even some good pictures and knickknacks.

Mr. Russell asked whether Mr. Knight thought that the CEO would be willing to donate some old furniture and equipment. Mr. Knight said that would be premature, but he indicated that his own office might have an old copier that at least was a little more modern than the thirteen-step, one-copy-at-a-time unit we have, for which the special paper is not made anymore.

Never one to leave a subject alone, Mr. Colberg added caustically, "Maybe that's why I never see financial reports anymore."

Despite some of the tone of our discussion, we found the group beginning to demonstrate both creativity and unity in dividing the tasks of finding or even donating old coffee machines, porch furniture, and wooden crates that could serve as file boxes.

Jack responded to several inquiries with assurances that he could provide receipts for fair-market value of such contributions and the participation expanded considerably. (Personally, I can't wait to see that old desk from Mrs. Lortz' basement that is suddenly worth $300!)

The question of artwork raised the problem that our walls are covered with pictures of the early days of the association and of the trip that Mr. and Mrs. Peter Paul Henderson took to Niagara Falls. Without thinking, Mrs. Greenlaw said that in terms of image, they should be the first to go, and everybody turned as one to where Mr. Peter Paul Henderson usually sits and gasped with relief that he wasn't there. It would have been a big one.

Having planned for most of the details, it was agreed to leave to the Personnel Committee all other general arrangements for the move. The only final instructions reflected the general good feeling around the table and our overall optimism about the future, because we instructed them to be sure to plan for expansion.

With the drums of sick green paint still in mind, Mrs. Buckminster asked what had become of our agreement to develop an ironclad conflict of interest policy. Mr. Yarborough apologized that he had not gotten to it but would get to work on it as long as it was understood that this wouldn't preclude his giving his wife, who is in the real-estate business, an inside track "now that we're finally talking about real money for a good office." Mr. Horton also cautioned the Board "not to be too shortsighted because, after all, it's the Board members who know the organization's needs and are often in the best position to give us good deals."

"Like the green paint?" Mr. Scala inquired.

Mr. Horton's reaction was a perfect match to our current color scheme.

Mr. Widen said that for once maybe we could shortcut an item and just adopt a policy that said, like other organizations do, that any time the association does business with a Board member, the item should be put up for bid, and it should be agreed in advance that the Board member would match the lowest bid. In that way, the association gets the best price, the Board member gets the business, and there's no real conflict.

That was about to sail through until Mr. Zukert said he "had to confess that that's the way it works in most organizations, but if you really think about it, who's going to bother bidding if they know the Board member is going to get the business anyway?"

That was a lot to think about, but because it was, we slowed down on the conflict of interest proposal and asked Mr. Yarborough to keep at it.

And then it was a good moment to have a break.

After we came back things still seemed good enough

that Mr. Zukert took the chance of asking if he could reintroduce the idea of a Board retreat, and Mr. Russell, with wariness, gave a cautious go-ahead. Mr. Zukert explained that with so much money likely to be flowing in from sales of services, bequests, United Way, and foundations, and with the need to prepare ourselves for the new surge of money and increased expectations inherent in the Program Committee's report, perhaps the time was at hand for us to take a good block of time to carefully think about the state of the organization and its long-term development. To his astonishment, Harriett Lortz was the first to agree. Asked why she had such a change of heart, she responded, "First, after tonight's meeting I'm feeling a bit more positive about things and even about people, so maybe it's worth the risk, but second, it's March and I've been in that damn house with those damn kids this whole damn dreary winter and I'll do anything to get out!"

For several minutes we busied ourself with ideas for the agenda, costs ("Thank goodness we don't need to worry about that kind of thing anymore," chimed several members), what to wear, when to have it, and that old bugaboo, where to have it. In such a spirit of camaraderie, it was agreed that we would leave the location to our Chairperson and Mr. Zukert, and then, as a liberated afterthought, to our Secretary also.

As to when, it was agreed that we ought not to put it off, but should "strike while the iron is hot . . . make hay . . . seize the day . . ." and such. So sometime in April, and definitely before our next regular meeting in May, was agreed on.

We were about to adjourn when someone realized that Mr. Wenski had not arrived. We knew he would be confused if he came and found us not in session. It was agreed that I would pin a note on the door which would explain our adjournment and give him a chance to sign in so he could get credit for attendance.

At that hour, and in that mood, *almost* no one seemed to want to bother with an executive session and the evaluation of the Executive Secretary. "Besides," said Mr. Scala resignedly, "you either like him or you don't, so what's to say?" Anyway, we all agreed that there would be plenty of informal opportunities to talk about people at the retreat. Jack said he thought he'd rather have our regular kangaroo court, but he wasn't taken seriously.

With that additional crisis passed, we adjourned at 11:37 P.M.

Respectfully submitted,

Mrs. Jeffrey (Effie) Black
Secretary of the Board of Directors

Notes from Our Board Retreat in April

We had agreed that we would meet by 4:00 P.M. to beat the traffic for our bus trip to Camp Bluebird, which we had rented for the weekend from the YWCA. The last of our group (Mr. Wenski!) arrived at 4:46, but only minutes after several others who were also tardy. The circumstances allowed them to feel slightly less guilty because the rented school bus didn't arrive until 5:14 ("On Fridays, I have to wait until baseball practice is over," said the driver). By that time, several needed to go to the bathroom (I didn't, but I wished I had) so we didn't actually get underway until just before 6:00.

There were some problems along the way.

Mrs. Mitchell's seven pieces of designer luggage had to be placed on top of everyone else's so they wouldn't get damaged, but in the rickety old bus they kept falling off until we agreed we'd take turns holding them in our laps.

The bus had no springs, which may be all right for children who are prehemorrhoidal, but made it difficult for our group. There was an ugly moment when Mrs.

Mitchell found out that Peter Paul Henderson was sitting on the bag he was supposed to be holding.

We weren't twenty minutes into our trip when it became obvious that the reason school buses are colored yellow is to blend with motion sickness.

Rev. Horsinger said that if he had ever known what the experience was like he would never have backed busing. Mr. Horton summarized it for all of us, "It's no wonder these kids have scrambled brains."

Our problem was compounded by many wrong turns, too many navigators, frequent pit stops, and one long debate with close vote on turning back.

Rodney Russell tried to lighten the situation by leading a sing-along, but it became obvious that the only song that everybody knew was "Row, Row, Row Your Boat" and after singing it eleven times and humming several others we sat silent and *sullen*. Besides, on that jarring ride, it wasn't safe to unclench your teeth.

When it became obvious that the trip was going to be a great deal longer than its advertised one and a half hours, Mr. Russell suggested that we use the time to advantage by beginning the evening's program with the orientation by our guest futurist, Waldo Wellington. Within moments, it was obvious it wouldn't work. At the first pothole, poor Mr. Wellington lost his uppers, and at the second his head almost went through the roof. Shaken and glazed, he muttered about his own future and refused to go on.

To get off the defensive, the driver imposed the "stay-seated requirement," and forewarned us that if he heard any more guff, he would exercise his authority to require quiet also. The only person allowed to stand was Jack Neal, who by this time had the state map totally unfolded and with each turn adjusted the map for the changing direction. Our route became so twisting and Jack was gyrating the map so wildly that he sliced five Board members and came close to injuring several others. We voted to proceed on concensus, which may have prolonged the trip but saved a lot of blood that would have included a lot of Jack's.

We finally arrived at 9:15 P.M., but our jubilation was short-lived. The only light in Camp Bluebird was a five-watt, stained, yellow bulb at the entrance, which revealed a note we would rather not have found. It seemed that the caretaker/cook had given up on us and gone home:

> If you do get here, women are upstairs in Dolley Madison on the left, and men are downstairs in Martha Washington on the right.
> Breakfast at 7–7:30 (no late arrivals served). Martha Washington's latrine is broken, so everybody should share Dolley Madison's.

At that moment the fact that there was at least one latrine working provided some solace, but Mr. Russell was faced with his first decision and crisis. He tried a vote of hands of those who needed to go badly, but it came out seven women and seven men. While our Chairperson tried to figure out what to do next the men headed for the woods, making the decision a great deal easier. There were complaints that some of the men had not gone far enough. "We could still hear you!"

While we were thus occupied the bus driver quietly unloaded our things. By the time we reassembled he was already halfway up the hill, leaving us no choice but to stay.

With the bus disappearing over the hill this weary group of pilgrims huddled together, waiting for leadership.

103

Mr. Colberg snarled, "This is more like survival camp."
Mr. Zukert added, "Like Outward Bound."

"Outward Bound is exactly what I was thinking of too," said Mrs. Lortz.

Mr. Russell led the trudge to Martha Washington and Dolley Madison respectively, and after setting up a schedule of male and female latrine watches, went into his dormitory, made up his cot, and pulled both the blanket and pillow over his head.

Some of us had worried that we might not wake up in time for the desperately needed but desperately brief breakfast. We needn't have worried. From 3:30 A.M. on, people began to crack out of the ice to test if they could still move. It wasn't long after that the lines outside the Dolley Madison latrine became long and unruly. Those on watch were swept aside by men and women who overnight had turned from uncivil to uncivilized. Mr. Russell rushed forward, still in his shorts, and though it was difficult to comprehend that this could be our leader, we kept our eyes on his face and not on his legs and tried to listen.

For a while it got terribly basic. We tried an alternation of boy/girl, boy/girl, but that didn't cover the situation adequately, so it came down to an interrogation of each person who was breaking through the lines, which went something like "How badly do you need to go?" and "How long do you think it will take you?"

Beyond that, there were some serious accusations that had to be worked through:

She didn't have to go anywhere near as bad as I did.
You could tell by the way she walked.

While the rest of us were in agony, she sat in there and did her nails.

Paul peed in the sink.

By this time it was already 7:15 and breakfast was half over, so Mr. Russell sent a delegation to negotiate with the caretaker/cook, who remained adamant that nothing would be served to anybody arriving after 7:30. We got around that by bringing trays to those for whom standing in line was more important than starving. These were errands of mercy which made us begin to feel warm, at least inside.

Breakfast was powdered eggs and bacon. Mr. Shapiro asked if any thought had been given to the dietary considerations of Jews in the group, and the caretaker/cook displayed momentary civility by offering to cook some sausage. He seemed hurt that his thoughtfulness had been rebuffed and he reverted to form.

There was no trouble getting people to the conference room on time, where a fire was being built. There was a stampede. Eight men and two women competed to build the best fire and were so quick about it that we already had an enormous blaze before it became obvious that the chimney had gotten stopped up over the winter. Each of us established his or her own endurance for how long the smoke could be tolerated while getting the benefit of the fire, but it wasn't long before all of us were back out in the cold watching the smoke and thinking of liability.

As volunteers we were enormously proud of how quickly the fire and rescue unit responded. They really saved our necks *and* Camp Bluebird. When we asked them how they had gotten there so fast, they explained that the Y had told them what kind of group was going to be there for the weekend and their total force was on full alert.

We thanked them profusely, but it became obvious that was not quite the end of it. Though it seemed somewhat unvolunteerlike, they made no bones of the fact that they usually get a minimum of $100 for this kind of service, so we took a collection and they went off with about $135. Mr. Knight offered them an extra $15 if they would take him with them but they just laughed, thinking he was kidding, and he cried, knowing he was not.

By then it was time for coffee and calisthentics, which seemed like a somewhat unusual combination. The reason became starkly obvious. It is absolutely necessary to keep that coffee moving through your system so it doesn't have a chance to settle in any one place, particularly your stomach.

It was coffee, leg squats, and out; coffee, pushups, and out; and coffee, sprints, and out, which at least got us warm.

At 10:30 we met again in the conference room with a stopped-up chimney and no fire. Mr. Scala thought he was being funny but was pretty much on the mark when he took a look at us and recited, "Give me your huddled masses yearning to be free."

Out of politeness we stayed settled for Waldo Wellington's glimpse into the future:

> Whenever we think about the future, it's generally defined as near-term, long-term, or the future generally. I like to talk about "forever."
>
> In forever, there will be more of most things and many more of some. Though the growth rates will be uneven, by the time we reach even the first stages of forever, there will be more babies, more young people, more adults, and more females. There will not be as

many males. Actually, there will be many fewer men for a long, long time. As women gain in dominance, they are likely to kill off most of the males. They will probably keep just enough locked up for artificial insemination and get rid of the rest. Sex will be passé. This will be the ultimate expression of liberation. Someday the pendulum may swing back, but not in the foreseeable forever.

Eighty-eight percent of the population will be beyond retirement age. There will be many more young old, old old, very old, and awfully old. In the farther reaches of forever the terribly old will begin to disappear. Medical science will have reached the point that nobody will visibly die, but the oldest of the old will get so shriveled and shrunken that they will just get lost.

Social Security will be taken out of the first $4 million of annual income, but benefits will begin at age nineteen. With cost-of-living adjustments compounded from now to forever, people will get $86,492 a month unless they have dependent children, in which case it will double. To support the aging population, child labor laws, a temporary fad of the 1900s, will be repealed and job training will be introduced as integral to neonatal parenting. The work week will be back up to one hundred hours a week. The service economy will have given way to a slave economy.

I am sad to have to tell this particular group that volunteers will be considered as enemies of the state. Anything that allows an individual to have personal influence on communities and societies will be considered antithetical to pure democracy, where everyone should have equal influence.

Research is already revealing that tolerance of even gradations of civility breeds unevenness in human behavior. In forever, everybody will be at their nastiest, which, despite its drawbacks, will mean that behavior will be far more predictable and life will be more on an even pace, albeit unbearable.

Sex change operations and mind-altering drugs will have also contributed to a more egalitarian society. During the typical life span, people will have an average of two and a three-eighths sex changes, and the state will administer periodic injections that will give everyone some sense of what it's like to be male, female, gay, poor, rich, old, infantile, tubercular, fat, happy, dead, depressed, and average. It will be the only time in the history of the world when we will know for a fact who is actually average.

During incipient forever, we will already have instantaneous communication with everyone. What started with a megaphone and progressed through wireless radio and the TV and reached its breakthrough with the car phone will reach a point where any of us can press a button and speak to everybody everywhere. The ultimate attraction will be that nobody can *not* listen. Gradually, that will induce a catatonic state in an increasing portion of the population, but that gets us beyond forever and into the new creation.

We will no longer have the basic index, now called Gross National Product—GNP. In its place, there will be ATMITW—All The Money In The World—but the object will still be the same, that is, each individual and nation will strive to get more of their share.

In the year 1985, what was then the U.S.A. had 18 percent of ATMITW, but by the year 2085, Mexico and its U.S. colony will be up to 23 percent.

The cost of carrying the U.S. debt will be the cause of the collapse of what is now known as the U.S.A. Long before forever, the cost of paying for the debt will have reached 100 percent of income and all other roles and services of government will have ceased. Civil libertarians will accept the blame for the government's going out of business, though they didn't plan it that way.

English will have been dropped as a second language, and even the Rockefellers and Mellons will have changed their names to Cortez and Hernandez so their children will fit in.

Head Start will be part of prenatal care.

Right-to-Lifers will still picket the Supreme Court, but there will be a difference, because the Catholics and Pro-Choicers will have switched sides, which will be explained by the new old science of gradualism.

Trade deficits will set a new record.

Corporate mergers will have reduced us to one multinational conglomerate called G.O.D.

Israel's inflation rate will be at 112,784 percent, but the Jews and Arabs will have reached harmonious agreement on all issues except borders, arms, and God.

One of the best features beyond the horizon is that everybody will be a leader, except, of course, adult males, who will have disqualified themselves in the preforever. Women and young people will take their turns at being mayor, governor, president, and czar for a day, and congressional terms will be for a week with no one allowed to succeed herself.

Women, who were never really interested in the boring regular seasons of men's sports, will have reorganized things so that in pro sports there will be nothing but play-offs all year round. Everything and everyone will be championship.

Perhaps one of the most encouraging prognostications for this group at this time is that through biofeedback, relaxation response, and other advanced forms of mind over matter, we will be able to control the temperatures of our bodies without regard to external climates.

Waldo tried to go on but was interrupted and engulfed with whistles, cheers, and shouts of, "Bring on forever!"
With that as background we thought about our own

future, which some people calculated might not last the day. Mr. Russell tried to whip us into more positive thoughts. He had quite wisely postponed his plan to use this session to have us let our hair down and let it all hang out. He had looked around at those gaunt, taut, desperate faces and thought the time for absolute license should be put off.

Lunch had been scheduled as a cookout, but it didn't take too much pleading to convince our keeper to move it indoors. It really didn't make much difference. It would have been inedible either way. To get that little extra warmth we had to sacrifice some of the benefit of the bird watcher's lecture. The camp dining room had small windows, and every time he would see a bird he'd shout something like, "There's a nuthatch!" But within fifteen minutes our necks had been snapped around so completely we suffered from collective whiplash. Ms. Trister said he wasn't very skilled anyway. He identified a robin as a cardinal, a turkey vulture as a seagull ("You can tell from the way he glides"), and a piliated woodpecker as a great blue heron. Her doubts were cinched when she asked, "How many life birds do you have?" and he replied, "Those that are flying or singing are all alive."

The lunch and program were followed by a bird walk, which may have been all right for young campers after the trails had been cleaned of winter debris, but for us it was too dangerous to look up. In just a half hour we had a sprained ankle, wrenched knee, pulled groin, slipped disc, not to mention incipient poison ivy and oak. When the casualties were all accounted for there was no escaping another emergency for the so-called volunteer unit and though it may not have seemed very caring, we asked them to hold their services under $100. Our first collection produced only $53.92, but Rev. Horsinger gave his

Thanksgiving week sermon and we collected just short of $91.00.

During our afternoon session our Chairperson gambled by suggesting that we were ready for some blue skying and asked people to speak their minds. We needed very little prodding.

"When will the other latrine be fixed?"

"How soon can we go home?"

"Let's draw straws to shoot the cook."

"Whose crazy idea was this?"

Looking at the positive side, Mr. Zukert, without reminding the group that it had been his idea, said, "If part of the purpose of the retreat is to wrench us out of our everyday considerations, then we are already having a particularly successful experience."

Mr. Fales spoke for all of us: "Shoot him *and* the cook!"

Mr. Russell pleaded with us to try to relate the blue skying to the organization, and there was an immediate response.

"Dissolve it," advised Mr. Shapiro. Mr. Russell chuckled but the point got the first serious consideration of the day.

Encouraged that things were taking a positive turn, Mr. Russell pushed his luck: "What are some way-out things we should think about to make the Board more effective?" But he was careful to ignore Jack Neal's outstretched hand. That became a bit obvious and awkward, because for at least three minutes Jack's was the only hand raised and for part of that time he had both hands waving frantically.

Finally, Mrs. Workenthrader saved the moment, but hardly the retreat, by suggesting that maybe our Board meetings would be a bit more orderly and productive if, like at her DAR lodge, we sat by seniority determined by office and years of service. She assured us this was just a "top-of-the-head kind of idea," but she produced a four-by six-foot blueprint that showed everybody's place, including exact years of service. Most of us were impressed, but Mr. Zukert muttered, "If this idea is what she comes up with after months of preparation, it's terrible to think what she might *really* brainstorm." Mr. Fales warmed to the idea and took it a step further. "Maybe we could even get chairs with our names on the back that we get to keep."

"Next thing you know someone will suggest we get jackets," snorted Mr. Colberg.

"Funny, I was just going to bring that up," said Mr. Widen.

For a moment it seemed that our brainstorming was spent but with nothing more substantial to latch onto, Mr. Scala picked up the thread and said that maybe we could be seated by some other pattern like liberals and conservatives or our voting records.

"How 'bout the good guys on one side and the bad guys on the other?" asked Mr. Horton sarcastically.

Before Mr. Widen could get his reaction together, Mr. Colberg interjected, "Too lopsided," and we sat and thought for quite a while longer. No new thought presented itself, so Mrs. Greenlaw said that maybe we could put a person's chair back a place each time a meeting was missed.

"Except for the officers, of course," said Mrs. Mitchell, and even I had to agree with her.

That at least got us on a slightly different topic involving Board attendance requirements, which, because of my own strong support, seemed to become our first important agreement. Unfortunately, Mrs. Mitchell derailed it with a filibuster that began, "If you're going to attract the *real* community leaders, you'll have to accept that we can't be as available as the rest of you," and ended much later with, "Quality is more important than quantity."

Mr. Zukert tried one last time by saying he "didn't mean to disagree with Mrs. Mitchell or to question the value of her very occasional participation, but he thought we should not overlook the values of continuity and demonstrated dedication." Mrs. Mitchell skewered him with a reminder that "you were the one who assured the corporate CEO that he would never have to attend meetings."

"Oh, he would be different," offered Mr. Zukert, but though most of us might agree with him in practice, he lost this one on a rare adherence to principle. (It would have been different if the CEO had accepted.)

Wishing to salvage *something* from our clouded blue skying, Mrs. Lortz suggested that we at least agree that a person who comes in more than an hour late shouldn't get credit for attendance. Mr. Knight reacted, "You mean Wenski has never been here!" And, with awareness that he no doubt had gotten the message, the matter was not pressed.

We moved to somewhat higher ground when Mrs. Pepper asked if we could review the day of the week scheduled for our meetings. As sometimes happens in such gatherings, the unanticipated comment brought the group alive, and for the next twenty minutes we were vital and vibrant. From day of the week it went to hour of the day, locations, whether meals should be served, order of the agenda, shape of the table, voting procedures, frequency of meetings, and enough other offerings that every single person was proposing, reacting, and interconnecting. Our retreat was finally in gear.

Tempo and spirit continued to build until Mrs. Mitchell, on behalf of the Personnel Committee, said that in fairness to working women we ought to consider having the meetings on Saturday mornings ("Whose side is she on anyway?" snapped Paula Masonowitz, not so sotto voce). Mr. Shapiro reminded the group that Saturday was the Jewish sabbath, and while he had the floor he pointed out that by holding rigidly to any one pattern we would frequently schedule meetings on Jewish holidays.

That set off Mrs. O'Reilly, who quickly gained the upper hand by an accusation that "you people of Jewish persuasion want every other day, and when we Catholics and some other real Christians give in, you take advantage of us by plunking the Annual Meeting on the one day we ask for, and on top of that you serve pot roast on Good Friday. . . ."

Seeing what an advantage she was gaining and that she was only just getting wound up, Mr. Shapiro thrust in, "I wasn't responsible but I'm willing to be the first to apologize. Also, I'll submit once again, as I have for each of the last four years, a list of sixteen of the days we respectfully ask the Board to avoid. In addition, it seems reasonable to ask you to avoid our sabbath."

You could tell by the reactions that most of the group found Mr. Shapiro pretty convincing, but logic and fairness are never matches for hysteria.

Mrs. O'Reilly rushed into the next round with, "We used to get all of Lent and then at least Holy Week, and now we're down to Good Friday and you're up to sixteen days, which will probably turn out to be sixty, so I think Saturdays are fair game. Besides, if you'd just move your day of worship to Sunday like the rest of us, we wouldn't have this problem."

"We were there first," jabbed Shapiro.

But she slugged back with, "There are twenty times more Christians than Jews, and besides, we take God more seriously than you do."

Mr. Shapiro said there was no sense discussing it

further because it was clear that prejudice rather than logic was being displayed.

That turned out to be a mistake.

"What do you mean by implying I'm against the Jews?" screamed Mrs. O'Reilly. "Some of my best friends are Jewish. I even suspect my butcher is Hebrew, but I would never want to say so without being sure."

"And you don't think you have a trace of prejudice?" howled Shapiro.

"No, what makes you think so?" counterpunched O'Reilly.

Rev. Horsinger finally succeeded in getting the combatants into their corners and proposed that we all agree that other than an occasional special event, such as this retreat, we would avoid Saturdays and Sundays and any special holidays that are called to our attention by any member of the Board.

Mrs. O'Reilly tried to have the last word when she seemed to agree with the solution but had to add, "We've got saints you've never even heard of and every blessed one of them has a day."

Mr. Shapiro was more gracious, "We'll miss you," he responded.

Mr. Russell called for a break.

Our caretaker/cook had prepared some painfully sour lemonade and then led us in vigorous calisthenics. Fortunately the rescue unit was still there, and on a per capita basis we were beginning to get our money's worth.

After the break, we were asked to think hard about our long-range plans. Mr. Russell began by suggesting that we review our current status and then consider where this might take us. "Before we know where we want to go, we have to know where we are now."

It was quickly apparent that even with the calisthenics and stomach pumping the mood had turned cold.

115

Mr. Yarborough snapped, "You ask us where we are now and where we want to go? We're at the coldest, dampest, dreariest deserted camp in all of North America and maybe even the world. So that covers where we are. As to where we want to get to, my sights are focused on getting home, and I'm highly motivated to do that. The sooner the better! So that covers the future, if there is any hope of having one. What else do you want to talk about?"

Mr. Russell thought that was a little negative, but he was wise enough not to take a vote on it. It was a small concession to avoid total mutiny when he said that we might shorten our Sunday-morning session and that he'd try to get the bus here so we could get an earlier start. It was something, but all in all he probably got only about as much credit as George Washington did when he said he'd stand while they crossed the Delaware to prove that it wasn't cold.

Ms. Trister said that she had an item left over from our discussion about the Board that could have some bearing on the future. She reminded the group, quite unnecessarily, that she was the newest and by far the youngest Board member (Mrs. Mitchell twitched) and said that she thought it would help us get along and do our collective job better "if Board meetings could be more interesting and stimulating, maybe even meaningful and fun."

The idea was so foreign that it was likely to hang out there and freeze, along with Beth Trister's enthusiasm, however naive. In grandmotherly fashion, Mrs. Buckminster explained that "serving on a Board is a lot like having a baby. The initial session involves anticipation and adventure, even if it doesn't live up to expectations, and all the rest simply ranges from nausea to cramps to pain, but it is what you produce that counts."

Ms. Trister and most of the rest of us were struck by that profound analogy.

Mr. Colberg spoiled the mood by commenting that, "So far, all we've done is lay an egg."

Mrs. Archer countered, "You men just don't understand, which is one of the reasons men don't make good Board members."

Mr. Russell reacted, "That seems like a rather sweeping generalization."

Mrs. Archer got into it by adding that she "wished you'd let us run this place by ourselves for just six months."

Penelope Mitchell beamed.

Mr. Colberg said, "So moved."

And we had to be reminded that we were just brainstorming.

Our Chairperson reminded us that our financial prospects seemed to be brightening. "Assuming that things go well with our bequest cultivation program, and our applications to United Way, and the Cutting Edge and Fail Safe Foundation, and several other things that seem to be popping, let's daydream together about what we might do with all that money."

"Go to a Marriott," chimed in Mrs. Pepper.

"Burn a camp," offered Mr. Scala.

"Merge with a good organization," offered Mr. Horton.

"Get a real exec," slipped in Mr. Colberg.

"Now we're getting to it," observed Mr. Russell, referring to the growing participation, but, with a narrower orientation, Jack Neal blanched.

"Get off probation," suggested Mrs. Mitchell.

"Pay off National," proposed Mr. Gonzalez.

Go it alone so we could forget probation and the debt in one fell swoop," chimed in Mr. Widen.

As happens in such discussions, one or two thoughts triggered related observations and that governs the flow of the discussion. In this case we were back into our old topic of "What do we get from National?" The litany that flowed from that question was not altogether positive. What we get are "cranky letters," "a lot of forms to fill out," and "a National meeting that costs an arm and a leg."

A few people were a bit more positive, reminding us, for example, that "we are part of an umbrella organization." Mr. Gonzalez suggested that "for those dues we could buy everybody a Golden Parachute."

"But we don't pay them anyway," scolded Mrs. Mitchell. But unfortunately she added, "And that leaves someone out in the cold." Her figure of speech did little to win her point.

Mr. Wenski reminded the group that we get the benefit of National's radio and TV coverage, but Mr. Fales responded, somewhat sarcastically, that he had to get up last Sunday morning about 3:45 A.M. for a bromoseltzer and "While I was waiting for its effect I turned on the TV and finally saw one of their spots."

Mr. Horton pointed out, "We have to weigh the value of National presence and National leadership." But it was not quite clear which side he was on.

Rev. Horsinger said we needed to be fair and had to ask ourselves, "What do they get from keeping us in?"

In the long silence that followed, you could tell we recognized it was pretty much of a standoff. That was usually where our discussions ended, except when we were considering repaying the back debt.

Mrs. Workenthrader suggested, "While we're talking about money and willing to leave ourselves open by offering what might turn out to be crazy ideas, maybe all of us should commit ourselves to raising at least two or three thousand dollars this next year for something like a Program Development Fund for New Ventures." The group was both startled and silent, but, when we recovered, the summary of the Board's reaction was that it was indeed a crazy idea and had put a crimp in anyone else's willingness to spout off the top of his head.

Mr. Widen, whose spout always seemed to be open anyway, asked the group to consider, "Why don't we form affiliates and make them pay us?" At first it seemed too crazy to talk about, but the more he went on the more the idea appealed. "We could do what National does to State and State does to us. Instead of having the buck stop here we can just pass it on to another layer."

It's a good lesson that you can never predict when and where the bright idea will emerge. How this had escaped us all these years was a bafflement. What we would do is to organize subunits at the community and maybe even neighborhood levels and assign them their work with a requirement that they give us twenty-five percent of everything they raise.

"We could even impose standards and put them on probation," gleamed Mr. Gonzalez.

"Won't the subunits expect a lot of services from us?" cautioned Mr. Colberg.

"We can just buck that on to State and National," chirped in Jack Neal, who was catching the spirit of it.

"And then the buck would stop at National," enthused Mr. Peter Paul Henderson, who was shaking with the delight of his evil thought.

"Maybe that's why they're setting up an international entity," observed Mrs. Mitchell.

The idea of going from a doer to an adviser, an imposer of standards and not a complier, a fund receiver and not a fundraiser gave us all such a sense of release that we felt spent but very good.

It was the right time to adjourn for our scheduled recreation.

Knowing his group by now, our caretaker/cook decided

that volleyball, horseshoes, bird walks, and his other planned activities were all too dangerous. On the other hand, he realized that if we just sat around, we would freeze to death and he might be liable.

Ms. Trister proved the point that she was indeed the youngest when she suggested hopscotch and jumprope, which seemed ridiculously juvenile, but once we got into it they were kind of fun and at least kept the blood going.

Mrs. Lortz and Mr. Scala swore it was an accident that Mr. Peter Paul Henderson's neck got caught in the jump rope. While he struggled, the knot seemed only to get tighter and we debated whether it was worth calling the rescue unit for just one person. We decided it wasn't because we were just about out of money and if he didn't make it we could try CPR and then call them if it didn't work because they usually got here in around ten minutes anyway.

Three of the more adventuresome souls did strike off for a hike and after about a half hour we got worried and two others volunteered to be a search party. After another half hour, when none of the five had showed up, we agreed to whistle and yell as loud as we could so that they would know where home base was. After about six minutes of the most awful cacaphony of blood-curdling screams, our friendly fire and rescue unit screeched in, and we knew it was time for a Saturday evening collection. Because we hadn't actually called them, we suggested twenty-five dollars. They said that because five people were involved it had to be at least fifty dollars. When we realized that meant ten dollars a head, Mr. Zukert wanted to know "Which five are they?" and, when told, refused to pay his fair share.

From old pants pockets, bottoms of purses, shoes, and even out of a bra or two, we scraped together $42.80, which they accepted and sped off on their errand of mercy.

It was remarkable that they were back in just twenty minutes with all five of our lost sheep safe, but sad to say, not sound. When we asked what had happened and how the unit had found our people so quickly, they said that it's routine on such Saturday night emergencies to go straight to Hardy's Tavern, which is not only what our original three had done but what the search party had duplicated, and by now all five did indeed look sheepish—and unsteady. The rule was that no liquor was allowed in the camp, but it was absolutely clear that our shifty-eyed little band had found a way to get around that. Even as horrified and humiliated as some of us felt, we could not help noticing how warm they looked.

One of the rescue unit personnel noticed that our Founder's head seemed to face backward and with our permission gave it a violent twist, which brought Mr. Henderson's eyes forward but not into focus. Two of us led him into the dining room.

The Y's promotion brochure said that Saturday night supper was "The Grand Splash," and if slop makes splash then I suppose they are right.

We tried to make light of it by having a guessing game as to what the basic ingredients were, but those that seemed to come closest only made the experience worse.

Several were hungry enough to try to gag it down, and as we looked around it was like a family liver night and: "Eat it or else!"

Ordinarily, I can survive by looking forward to dessert and coffee, but with breakfast and lunch in recent memory, I joined the gaggers.

After dinner, we joined together in the assembly room for a night of the kind of togetherness that forges a permanent bond among strangers.

Based on our experience on the bus, we decided to skip the scheduled sing-along and, based on this noon's lecture on birds, we decided to skip the young man's lecture on bark and moss. We went right to the one thing we had all been looking forward to this long day—and that was the movies. At our last Board meeting, we had a prolonged discussion about what films to show and had found that the common denominator was cartoons.

While eleven people participated or advised in the setting up of the projector, the rest of us got the chairs unfolded and organized. These group activities absorbed about three-quarters of an hour and, just when we were ready to go, everyone noticed that Jack Neal had not set the screen up, but it turned out the reason Jack had not set the screen up yet was that Jack Neal had forgotten the screen. The disappointment of older people is far greater than that of younger people when Saturday night's movies are taken away.

When no one came forward with a solution, Mr. Russell volunteered to use his sheet, and when he observed that "it might warm it up anyway," nineteen volunteers came forward. By the time they were all pinned up we could have had panoramic vista vision.

When we were finally ready to go, Mr. Gonzalez turned off the lights with a flourish which made it somewhat obvious that he also turned off all the power in the room. It took fifteen minutes to figure out that maybe we could unscrew most of the bulbs, and there was even some envy for those who burned their hands. With all that behind us we settled in for our cartoons. The first short ones were about Donald Duck and Woody Woodpecker and put us all in a better mood. We needed all the positive reserve we could muster for what came next.

In retrospect, we figured it had to be innocence that caused Jack to pick the full-length Felix which he swore was listed as both a cartoon and as educational. Had he looked just a little further, he would have found it listed more prominently as "Adult," "X," and "Hard Porn."

With the two funny short subjects behind us, the conversation was chipper as we settled in for a whole forty-five minutes of Felix the Cat. What was funny was that it took us so long to figure out that it wasn't funny. One of the men admitted later that he knew in an instant what was coming but hadn't dared to admit he had already seen it. That's the opposite of courage.

It was obvious that night that self-fulfilling prophecy really does work. We were so prepared to be amused that the first time Felix mated, even Mrs. O'Reilly was laughing uproariously, and it wasn't until Felix began a ménage à trois that her howls turned to gasps, and either through an undersupply of oxygen or an oversupply of humiliation she passed out very cold. Each time we revived her she came to only long enough to remember and went out again. We were scared enough about her that we called the volunteer fire and rescue squad. While waiting for them we prayed for Mrs. O'Reilly. We also prayed that her Medicare would cover the "contribution," and we prayed that our "volunteers" would accept an IOU.

When she was finally brought around enough to stay around, we sat together like a stunned hunting party that had started out for rabbits and had encountered a herd of elephants. It was one of those moments in life when a whole group is literally, actually, truly, and in fact speechless. It was group shock.

The pall was finally broken by the one person who hadn't seemed to share in it. He was the *same* person who had seemed to share most deeply in the events of Hardy's Tavern. Mr. Wenski never changed that faraway grin until he finally realized the film had gone off and wasn't coming back on again.

Sunday breakfast was awful, and it wasn't just the food. No one looked at one another, which meant we had to look straight at the food, which was a cold lumpy oatmeal that looked back with a dare that few of us challenged. God willing, tonight we'd be home for real food.

To everyone's surprise, there was a 100 percent attendance at our nondenominational service. With the events of the previous evening starkly with us we prayed very hard. Jack Neal prayed hardest of all.

Rev. Horsinger spoke meaningfully on the evils of the flesh but said God was understanding of people who are exposed to sin against their wishes. He said it would only be a problem for those who looked even after they knew what they were looking at. Several prayed harder, and Mrs. O'Reilly wanted me to be specific about when she had passed out.

When we began our last session, Mr. Colberg suggested that we begin with an executive session, but Rev. Horsinger reopened his sermon with emphasis on forgiveness and when Jack bowed his head some of us were fearful that too much blood would rush into it. Mr. Colberg said it would be the only time we could be sure something was in it.

Mr. Russell reminded the group that we had all been asked to read Brian O'Connell's *The Board Member's Book* in preparation for the retreat and particularly for this session. He asked for reactions to the book. It was clear it was going to be a slow morning. Mr. Scala finally pointed out that he was slow getting to it and when he started into it the night before he had fallen asleep before getting too far. Several others agreed that this had been their experience also. Mr. Zukert pointed out, in his wise way, that, when people are that cold and miserable and have had such an upsetting experience, if any one book can put such a group to sleep then it must be considered a very valuable resource.

Mrs. Lortz said, "We ought to start every Board meeting with it."

Mr. Russell asked, "Is that all you got out of it?" and Mr. Yarborough seemed to speak for all of us when he responded, "So far."

Not getting far in that direction and feeling a little safer because the retreat was beginning to wind down, our Chairperson asked if any of us had any concerns we would want to bring up in this candid, safe atmosphere.

Mr. Fales expressed the concern that someone had used his toothbrush, which he had left in the latrine. Finally, Mr. Widen "fessed up" but offered the assurance that he had only used it as a nail brush.

Mrs. O'Reilly expressed concern about how she was going to confess the night's film experience, and Rev. Horsinger agreed to call Father Scallon to lay the groundwork. "Just one thing," she implored, "Don't tell him it happened at a retreat."

Mr. Horton stood to make a point which drew our attention in this otherwise informal gathering. "Perhaps I'm the only one who can't take it, but I have to ask, do we absolutely have to have lunch?" He gagged as he finished, and all around the room shoulders hunched and shook in the same telltale retch. Jack Neal settled the matter by announcing, "It's already paid for." You can't argue with that, or at least I didn't think so.

Suddenly, Mr. Scala put a fist in the air and with rebellion in his eyes announced, "I can't do it, I won't do it, and even if we can't be reimbursed we shouldn't put ourselves through it again."

Mr. Gonzalez misread the uprising by commenting, "Didn't you hear what Jack said? It's already paid for."

Revolution swept the room. As unbelievable as it

seemed, the Board was about to be independent and creative and not eat our caretaker/cook's Sunday lunch. The freedom from that action and the exhilaration of our boldness carried us to new heights. Mrs. Pepper even suggested we leave early and go to McDonalds.

The cheers were deafening. That is, until we realized we had no money. Mr. Zukert suggested we try to borrow some from the volunteer fire and rescue unit. "They've got lots of it," he said. But nobody dared.

Finally, with initial hesitation but growing confidence, Penelope Mitchell stammered that she had withheld her mad money and "do you think fifty dollars would buy lunch?"

Some were surprised and hurt that she had held out on us, but I explained that, with her personality, mad money is a pretty essential commodity. In any case the news and realization that we were not going to have lunch here and had money to go to McDonald's and were leaving right away all lifted the group in rejoicing (and no doubt lifted Mrs. Mitchell's chances of being our next Chairperson).

The only item of business left was to call the rescue unit so they would know they had the rest of the weekend off. They said they'd wait until we were out of sight.

With all those decisions behind us and what was clearly a successful retreat under our belts, we packed and helped one another onto the bus and "rowed, rowed, rowed our boat" from Camp Bluebird toward McDonalds and home.

Respectfully submitted,

Mrs. Jeffrey (Effie) Black
Secretary of the Board of Directors

Minutes of Our May Board Meeting

The meeting was opened at 8:30 P.M., because we kept waiting, hoping that Mr. Gonzalez would arrive with the Treasurer's report.

"The coward's not going to show up," shouted Mr. Shapiro.

"Maybe he's coming with Mr. Wenski," suggested Mrs. Pepper.

"We can't wait that long!" exclaimed Mrs. Greenlaw.

Mr. Russell could tell he had a tougher than usual meeting on his hands and moved aggressively to take charge. "I assure you all, we *are* going to have a Treasurer's report, even if Mr. Gonzalez doesn't show up. We'll give him another half hour and then ask Jack to review the financial statements for him. I also assure you that we *are* going to have the executive session to review the Executive Secretary's performance." Jack interrupted imploringly, "Do you think it's fair to ask me to do the Treasurer's report *and* still have my evaluation?"

"Sounds like a perfect combination," responded Mr. Colberg eagerly.

With that, Mr. Russell returned to the proper order of business and called for a reading of the minutes of our last meeting. Perhaps it was because the minutes had been a source of so much upset the last time or perhaps it was a reflection of important business still to come, but in any case there was no discussion of the minutes. Mr. Russell was so taken with surprise that he remained occupied with his pocket calculator for a good ninety seconds before it suddenly hit him that there was absolute silence in response to the minutes. He explained that he had settled in to do his monthly expense report and apologized that he didn't realize that something was wrong.

Mr. Russell acknowledged that the retreat had not quite served the purpose of team building and camaraderie but thought we might rebuild some of our prior togetherness if Mrs. Pepper would apologize to Mrs. Archer, and Mrs. Archer would apologize to Mr. Colberg, and Mr. Colberg would apologize to both Mrs. Greenlaw and Mr. Scala, and if Mrs. Greenlaw and Mr. Scala would apologize respectively to Rev. Horsinger and Mr. Fales, and if Rev. Horsinger and Mr. Fales would apologize to each other. The awkward nods across the table with eyes averted from the object of one's contriteness would hardly be characterized as a foot-thumping catharsis, but Mr. Russell took what he could get and returned to the regular order of business.

Ms. Trister said that she has now attended an orientation session, six Board meetings, an Annual Meeting, and a Board retreat and had learned a lot about the other Board members and the founding of the organization, but

"I have to confess that I am still not absolutely sure what the organization *really* does."

Mrs. O'Reilly responded reassuringly, "Not to worry dear, I've been here three years and I'm not sure, either. But it finally stops bothering you. You get caught up in the organization itself and just begin to ride with it."

Mr. Russell looked around and, not spotting the Treasurer, asked Jack Neal if he would summarize our financial position. White as a sheet, Jack pleaded, "Mr. Gonzalez still has twelve minutes."

"In that case, let's undertake the executive session," suggested Mr. Russell.

"Do you have to call it an undertaking?" implored Jack, whose pale white had become a spottled blue green with a few patches of bruised pink.

"I assure you, we'll give you your just due," comforted Mrs. Mitchell. "Perfectly said," topped Mr. Shapiro.

As Jack and his Office Manager, Administrative Assistant, Assistant Secretary, and Assistant Treasurer, Paula Masonowitz, left the room, the Board members rearranged their chairs into a tight circle, and with each scrape of a chair, Jack's stomach got tighter, too. When he reached the door, Paula helped him through.

Before we actually began, Mr. Russell had me peek out of each door to be sure Jack wasn't listening in.

The discussion started positively enough. For the first several minutes there was silence. In the next ten minutes there were some nice things said. For example, both Mr. Yarborough and Mrs. Archer commented on how hard Jack works. Mr. Zukert responded, "I know he works hard, but I'm not sure what he does all that time."

If it's not confusing metaphors, from that point the roller coaster started down and the fur began to fly. Twice I had to go out and ask the staff to move farther away so they wouldn't hear the shrill voices.

This being an executive session, the minutes don't have to be as complete as I'm generally noted for, but, for future reference, I will provide: 1) some flavor of the discussion, 2) a summary of the points we seemed to agree on, and 3) our conclusion.

1. *Flavor*

Some people like him and some don't.

In the past, Jack has expressed the view that Mr. Colberg and Mr. Shapiro are out to get him. It's true.

It's not that a lot of people actively dislike Jack or disapprove of what he does. There's just a vague sense of his worthlessness.

On balance, he has his defenders, but when pressed for specifics, they tend to point out things like "Nice teeth," or "Not many people in these jobs went to prep school," or "You don't remember the last one!"

2. *Generally Agreed Observations*

We want an Executive to take charge, but not usurp the Board's responsibilities and prerogatives.

Our Executive should be a more forceful spokesman for the organization but not get out front.

An Executive should come to committee and Board meetings with crisp recommendations for all the action items, but should not talk too much.

A good Executive should spend more time in the office "and less on all that outside junk."

"Jack should get out and do more and not spend all his time behind that big desk."

A good Executive should be more confident and aggressive but definitely not assertive.

We need a real leader who can tell us what to do and

make us do it but know his subordinate place in the organization.

He should look more like an Executive ("If only we could get him to wear suits with vests"), but he should come across more as a charity worker ("Maybe I can find him an old cross to wear," Rev. Horsinger volunteered).

We need someone who has skills in fundraising, management, organizing, budgeting, PR, program direction, public speaking, planning, evaluation, proposal writing, office management and community networking and who has such personal attributes as leadership abilities, pleasant manner, good looks, unflappability, and the ability to get along with everybody ("Maybe I could find an even larger cross that he can carry!" concluded the Reverend).

To be fair, we agreed that it is unreasonable to want our Executive to have *all* these skills and qualities, but there was considerable disagreement about what qualities Jack has.

"He doesn't have a damn one!" accused Mr. Shapiro.

"That's not fair," protested Mrs. Workenthrader.

"Name two," challenged Mr. Colberg.

Mrs. Workenthrader stumbled slightly but finally blurted out, "Well at least he comes to all the meetings." But no sooner was it out that she realized that some might spot a negative in it. She started to try again, but the flow was against her.

3. Our Conclusions

After about an hour of scalding candor, during which I twice went out to assure Jack that we were just into some miscellaneous matters off the track, our Chairperson said it was time to try to pull it all together. This was not altogether well received. Some were clearly enjoying the free spiritedness of the trial and others were uncomfortable with what it might lead to. Finally, Mr. Fales stepped in with, "There's no sense in cutting him up anymore. It's pretty obvious we have to let him go."

More than half the Board members were on their feet protesting that Fales had totally misread the discussion. Mrs. Mitchell was heard above the others crying, "Oh my God, that's not what we've been saying at all. We've just been adding up all his faults and shortcomings and just because there are so many of them doesn't mean we would be disloyal to him."

Mr. Colberg tried to be analytical. "If we had been keeping a tally with his strengths on one side and weaknesses on the other, we'd have thirty-two pages of black marks and only nice teeth going for him."

"Don't forget 'working hard,' " added Mrs. Pepper.

"Maybe the problem is we don't pay him enough," said Ms. Trister. "You know, it's a proven fact that people respond positively to confidence and fairness."

"I can't believe this," said Mr. Colberg apoplectically, but his analytical approach was giving way to the mysticism of collective judgment, where kind hearts and cold feet outweigh logic every time.

While four people were on their feet protesting that the discussion required bold action, the majority formulated a motion which would give Jack a 10 percent raise while putting him on probation until at least a few of his gross inadequacies showed evidence of turnaround.

The warring between a clear majority and an intransigent minority might have gone on indefinitely, but it was at that moment that Mr. Gonzalez showed up, and Mr. Russell seized the diversion to declare a sense of the meeting and called for a recess "while we regroup for Gonzalez." It was probably true that our Treasurer had not turned up earlier out of fear of the consequences, for he responded to our Chairperson's "regrouping" with stark terror in every line of his face.

Sometimes a short recess is called a comfort break. This was not one of them. Perhaps the most uncomfortable was Jack Neal, who was told only that the executive session had ended so we could take up the Treasurer's report. Compared to him, Mr. Gonzalez was a model of composure.

It was clear at the start that bad news was coming when Mr. Gonzalez began with the reminder that "it's not fair to shoot the messenger." We also knew we were in trouble when Mr. Gonzalez kept referring to himself as our banker and not as our Treasurer. The last time that happened, every Board member had to pony up his or her share of the overdraft.

I'll say this for our Treasurer, he didn't mince words. He put it to us this way:

"Ladies and gentlemen, you have been clobbered by a triple whammy.

> "One. The Cutting Edge and Fail Safe Foundation has turned you down because the organization is not well enough established with a proven track record.
>
> "Two. The United Way has turned you down because this is not an emerging organization.
>
> "Three. No bequest has come in because nobody has died yet who believes the organization is beyond 'emerged' but still 'unproven.' "

Each of these was given with escalating gravity, pitch, tremor, and timbre, ending in what started out to be one of our Treasurer's classic solos.

"You are broke, zeroed out, creditless, down the tube, penniless . . ." But by the time he was well into his performance, it had become triple harmony with our

Chairperson trying to shut him up and with the Board adding its own response so that it began to sound like a funeral dirge.

"You are indebted.
                    OK, OK, we hear you.
                                        Oh, my God.

You are destitute.
                    OK, OK, that's enough.
                                        What will happen
                                        to us?

You are ruined.
                    Please, you've made your point.
                                        We're all liable.

You are on the street.
                    We've got your message loud and
                    clear.
                                        Can they attach
                                        our homes?

You're bottoms up.
                    Stop it, Harry.
                                        That's what comes
                                        from being volun-
                                        teers."

But neither Mr. Russell nor the full Board were a match for the person posing for a Treasurer in banker's clothing. "You're through, finished, awash in red ink, bad risks, fiscally embarrassed, financial bummers, the wolf's at the door . . . ," until he dropped exhausted into his seat and the whole congregation wept with the physical exertion and meaning of it all.

Mr. Zukert was the first to recover and pleaded, "It's

really *that* bad?!" But when Mr. Gonzalez started to get to his feet, Mr. Russell cut him off with words that shall not be included in *my* minutes.

Mrs. Lortz asked our Treasurer if he "had a ballpark figure as to what it would cost each Board member to make things right?"

"In the neighborhood of ten to fifteen thou."

And this time the responses from the chorus outlasted any litany that even Mr. Gonzalez could string together. It was at this point that Mr. Wenski arrived and profusely begged forgiveness: "I was collecting door to door for the Cancer Society and just kept getting into long conversations."

"How much did you get?" asked Mrs. O'Reilly.

"Forty-one dollars and seventy-five cents," beamed a curious Mr. Wenski.

"Put it on the table along with everything else you've got," demanded Mr. Horton.

"What is this, a hold-up?" asked incredulous Mr. Wenski.

"Far worse, much worse, a thousand times worse," started Mr. Gonzalez, but Mr. Russell broke in and explained the situation to our late arrival, whose blanched, drained panic now blended in with everyone else's.

We realized that our "retreat" had not begun to test our creative thinking. With our backs to the wall, we would somehow raise the money.

One scheme seemed to offer a sure out. Mrs. Lortz explained the way a lot of the rich agencies get their money is to testify before the county board and sometimes even at the state legislature on behalf of the government agency that is their counterpart, like the health agency and health department. By being the government agency's citizens' lobby, appropriations are protected and usually increased, and then the voluntary group applies for just a tiny fraction for its own work, which is, of course, to be the citizens' lobby.

"Oh, I know all about that," said Mr. Zukert. "Some organizations have even carried it to the extreme of an informal agreement that they get 1 percent of the appropriations."

"I hear the Headache Society is up to two and seven-eighths percent," joined Mrs. Workenthrader.

"What happens if the citizens' lobby wants to cut appropriations or doesn't think its government counterpart is doing a good job?" cautioned Rev. Horsinger.

"And cut off its lifeline?" scoffed Mr. Wenski, now totally caught up in the practicalities.

"Could this be called lobbying?" tested Mr. Colberg.

"A few get into trouble, but most cover it under public education," assured Mrs. Archer.

"And what if someone uncovered the fact that we were involved with a quid pro quo?" persisted Rev. Horsinger.

"Nobody said anything about the Mafia," reacted Mrs. O'Reilly.

Undeterred, the Reverend bore in. "But wouldn't it look terrible if we were found to sell our testimony for a fixed portion of the agency's appropriation?"

"Oh, it's nothing that obvious," assured Mrs. Archer. "It's just understood that your applications get fair treatment that happens to average out around one percent."

"I still don't like it," our moralist entoned. "There's nobody more hard pressed than I to even dream of coming up with fifteen thousand dollars, but it's one thing to go to jail as a pauper and another to get sent there for a shady scheme."

Mrs. Archer responded with shrieks of injured honor, but the prospect of double jeopardy was beginning to sober the discussion.

Back at the point of "lobbying," Mr. Peter Paul Henderson had come alert but with his neck injuries it had taken until now for him to speak. When he did, it was with one of those statements that put matters to rest. "We don't do lobbying," he concluded, and for the time being at least, that income possibility was closed. It was clear, though, that our Founder, First Chairperson, and Chairperson Emeritus may have greased the skids for his departure.

Though at first it didn't seem like an adequate response to a crisis, we found ourselves back on the old subject of a Special Event.

The idea of a dance or ball was resurrected, but got little more enthusiasm than it had in the past. "Besides," I said, "My husband would be a little suspicious if so soon after the retreat, I told him we had decided to have a dance. He is still probing what went on out at Camp Bluebird."

"Why is it, so many other organizations make so much money on their society balls," wondered Mrs. Greenlaw.

Jack Neal responded thoughtfully, "It helps to start with a Board that glitters with names, money, and connections," and was in trouble all over again.

"Didn't we once try a walkathon?" asked Mr. Horton. "Yes, I'm afraid we did," replied Mr. Russell, "and further, I'm afraid we set it on the same day and track as the Leukemia Society's bikeathon and so many of our people got run down and cut up, it cost us more than we made."

"We seem to be good at that," added Mr. Gonzalez.

Undiscouraged, Ms. Trister said that maybe we should try one of the current gimmicks that involves a "non-event," where you assure someone they don't have to go to a stuffy ball or some other special event, and, out of appreciation and charitable impulse, they contribute the same amount of money and often much more.

Mr. Colberg said that "it sure would fit our pattern of activities where nobody shows up anyway."

Mrs. Mitchell splashed the final cold water by saying that by the time she had come to the organization, we had such a reputation for nonevents that we'd best not call unfortunate attention to ourselves.

Again, out of the innocence of newness and attractive enthusiasm, Ms. Trister asked if we had ever tried a chili cookoff, but the second she saw Mr. Peter Paul Henderson's face go pale and jaw go slack, she regretted it.

Fortunately the moment passed and with it any further bright ideas, so Mr. Shapiro said that maybe we would just have to kick in the money, which stimulated a lot of violent body language, if not brainstorms.

As inevitably happens in such discussions, someone recalled our last carnival and made the mistake of mentioning it. Though it was six years ago, events are still too recent and raw to be remembered with anything like nostalgia or humor. Some circumstances had taken us a long time to overcome, like the mayor and his wife getting stuck on top of the Ferris wheel, the school superintendent being hit in the fanny by a dart that missed a balloon by 180 degrees, the wind tunnel blowing the hairpiece off the president of the chamber of commerce, and the chief of police claiming to have gotten pyorrhea from our kissing booth.

With surprising insensitivity, Mr. Shapiro suggested Bingo, but Mrs. O'Reilly scotched that by assuring the group that "Father Scallon would be absolutely furious and I have enough trouble getting through his confessions without a two hour novena as it is."

Our always creative head of the Public Relations Committee, Pat Greenlaw, came up with the novel idea of a scavenger hunt, but she inadvertently stepped on her own idea when she suggested that we could include a search to find the first person ever served by our organization.

Mrs. Lortz said, "That might get rather expensive because we'd probably have to give everybody a shovel."

"That's not fair!" screamed Mr. Peter Paul Henderson.

"Besides," seconded Jack Neal, "our services have gotten much better."

It was another example of a good idea being lost with a bad "for instance."

We covered the ground of bake sales, art auctions, and about every conceivable product or service we might peddle. Someone else was already doing it, or we had tried it and failed, or the investment made it too risky for even this desperate group.

We covered grapefruit, flowers, dishes, casseroles, cookies, candy, Bibles, magazines, airplane rides, and every conceivable fruit, vegetable, sweet, or adventure, but someone was already there.

Next we tried the tack of special days, but someone has beaten us to Valentine's Day, Thanksgiving, Easter, Christmas, and, according to the clearinghouse calendar, 850 other days of the year. The discussion was somewhat useful, though, because we thought of some things we might do for our bequest program on Memorial Day ("While you're remembering, remember us"). Someone had the novel idea of using people's birthdays ("Make our day—pass up your day") but even though we agreed there was a germ of an idea there, we couldn't quite make it flower.

We were probably only an inch away from having to face putting up the money ourselves when Mr. Yarborough saved the day. He reminded us that in our discussions about networking and about applying to the United Way and to the Cutting Edge and Fail Safe Foundation we kept learning that our program falls between the slats of what other people are doing. He reminded us that we had come to realize that what we are trying to do has implications for art museums, high blood pressure, youth services, preservation, the elderly, unemployment, international understanding, and protection of the ozone layer, to name a few. "Wouldn't it make sense, then," he spun out with fascinating logic, "if we give up trying to raise money ourselves but simply ask all the organizations that already raise money for these causes to give us a piece of what they raise. With the breadth of our interest, we wouldn't have to ask for much. I've not really thought it out, but for organizations where there is a good deal of overlap, we could ask for maybe a third, and where it's only tangential, maybe as little as two or three percent."

"What if they won't give it to us?" asked Mr. Gonzalez pessimistically.

"I think they'll see the logic of it," interjected Mrs. Pepper.

"It's absolutely logical, and if they don't agree cooperatively," warmed Mr. Scala, "we could politely suggest that we might have to conduct our own fundraising campaign for the same cause in the same week and that should bring them around."

"This puts a whole new light on the concept and term 'our fair share,'" said Mr. Knight optimistically. "We could even call the campaign 'Our Share from Your Share.'"

"I can remember the meetings when we sat around worrying about how much of what we were trying to do overlapped with some of the larger groups already in the community," put in Mrs. O'Reilly. "But with this concept, the more the overlap the more we can charge." Mrs. Archer chimed in, "Our campaign theme could be 'Pay Your Overlap.'"

"And," enthused Pat Greenlaw, "it would look great in publicity to say that we worked in cooperation with the

Red Cross, Crippled Children's Society, Nature Conservancy, YMCA, Council on Alcoholism, Jewish Federation, Mental Health Association, Meals on Wheels, Asia Society, Planetary Society, Presbyterian Hospital, and the United Negro College Fund. This is really big. This is absolutely fantastic."

Doubter Colberg, always the old stick-in-the-mud, still questioned whether these organizations would be that amenable or could be persuaded to give up some of their hard-won contributions, but Mr. Knight said, "We might just have to play hard ball." He said we'd have to go after the easiest ones first and with successes behind us we could then mow down the tougher ones. He even predicted that by the time we got our fair share of even half the groups with whom we overlap that we'd be bigger than the United Way and maybe even bigger than the Cutting Edge Foundation and Fail Safe. With renewed confidence, Mr. Wenski shouted, "Yeah, who needs them anyway!"

Rev. Horsinger cautioned that our methods sounded as though they might border on blackmail or extortion, and he shuddered when we progressed to such terms as "mowing them down."

Mr. Knight hastened to say that, while some might describe our intentions as skimming and we had to be prepared to go to the mat with some of the folks, it was all in the name of charity. He also reminded the Reverend and the group as a whole that as a Board we have a legal and moral responsibility to serve our organization.

The enthusiasm reached such a pitch that the group decided that perhaps we should try to knock off one of the big ones first, both to put ourselves on the map and not incidentally to solve the immediate shortfall. Mr. Fales was bold enough to suggest the Girl Scouts and there was a collective gasp. That really tested our resolve and caused not a little review of our prospects. It was one thing to talk about the Symphony or even Saint Luke's Orphanage, but the ultimate in daring was to think of putting the arm on the Girl Scouts.

We were given a bit more courage with examples of how we could subtly suggest cutting into their sales or switching our backing to Campfire, and, gradually, our feet tingled with the itch to take them on.

As with all such crusades we gained confidence from a marching song that Ms. Trister quickly composed. Within moments all of us had mastered the first stanza and, while she scribbled out the next ones, we circled the table, chanting:

> Scare a Scout
> Skim the Scouts
> Sis boom ba
> Our Organization
> Rah Rah Rah

Mr. Peter Paul Henderson was not able to march with us but he was clearly with us in spirit. With his eyes on the horizon and a drumbeat in his heart, he dared to whisper: "Maybe, just maybe, we could do the Knights of Columbus next."

On that note of optimism, the meeting was adjourned at 11:16 P.M.

Respectfully submitted,

Mrs. Jeffrey (Effie) Black
Secretary of the Board of Directors